Navigating the Internet of Things in the 22nd Century - Concepts, Applications, and Innovations

Edited by Muhammad Usman Tariq

Published in London, United Kingdom

Navigating the Internet of Things in the 22nd Century - Concepts, Applications, and Innovations
http://dx.doi.org/10.5772/intechopen.1004512
Edited by Muhammad Usman Tariq

Contributors
Alberto Camarero-Orive, Asrat Mulatu Beyene, Cajetan M. Akujuobi, Faith Nwokoma, Javier Vaca-Cabrero, Marija Prchkovska, Nicoletta González-Cancelas, Olivera Petrovska, Samuel W. Kibret, Samuel Zeyede Tefera, Steven C. Lindo, Vesna Knights

First published in London, United Kingdom, 2025 by IntechOpen
IntechOpen is the global imprint of INTECHOPEN LIMITED, registered in England and Wales, registration number: 11086078, 167-169 Great Portland Street, London, W1W 5PF, United Kingdom

For EU product safety concerns: IN TECH d.o.o., Prolaz Marije Krucifikse Kozulić 3, 51000 Rijeka, Croatia, info@intechopen.com or visit our website at intechopen.com.

British Library Cataloguing-in-Publication Data
A catalogue record for this book is available from the British Library

Navigating the Internet of Things in the 22nd Century - Concepts, Applications, and Innovations
Edited by Muhammad Usman Tariq
p. cm.
Print ISBN 978-1-83769-881-3
Online ISBN 978-1-83769-880-6
eBook (PDF) ISBN 978-1-83769-882-0

If disposing of this product, please recycle the paper responsibly.

Meet the editor

Dr. Muhammad Usman Tariq is a distinguished professional with over sixteen years of experience in academia and industry, focusing on integrating artificial intelligence (AI) and emerging technologies in higher education. As a leading expert in research and case studies, Dr. Tariq has worked in private and public sectors across the United States, Asia, and the Middle East, serving as a practitioner, facilitator, trainer, supervisor, consultant, researcher, assessor, online tutor, and counsellor. His first inventor status on four scientific patents showcases his dedication to research and innovation. His intellectual contributions include more than 300+ articles, case studies, and book chapters. Dr. Tariq advocates for AI's transformative potential in higher education, having published numerous research articles, reviews, and book chapters exploring AI applications and implications in teaching, learning, and administration. His research interests encompass AI-driven personalization, online and self-paced learning, student and faculty engagement, and the ethical considerations of AI in education. He is a Chartered Fellow at the Chartered Institute of Personnel and Development (CIPD), Principal Fellow of Advance HE UK, Senior Fellow of SEDA, Senior Member of IEEE, and a Certified Business and Management Educator.

Contents

Preface

The rapid evolution of technology and the proliferation of connected devices have positioned the Internet of Things (IoT) at the forefront of transformative innovations. This edited volume, *Navigating the Internet of Things in the 22nd Century – Concepts, Applications, and Innovations* aims to provide readers with a comprehensive understanding of IoT's dynamic landscape. The chapters in this book delve into various facets of IoT, exploring its potential, challenges, and the groundbreaking applications reshaping industries and societal frameworks.

In the opening chapter, *From Sensors to Smart Decisions: Building an Intelligent Irrigation System with Machine Learning*, the authors explore the intersection of IoT and artificial intelligence to tackle agricultural challenges. This chapter underscores the critical role of machine learning in enhancing irrigation systems, leading to optimal resource utilisation and sustainability. Through intelligent decision-making models, this work exemplifies the potential of IoT-driven agriculture to mitigate resource scarcity and improve yields.

Enhancing Smart Parking Management through Machine Learning and AI Integration in IoT Environments, the focus of the second chapter presents a cutting-edge approach to urban mobility challenges. With urbanisation accelerating, efficient parking solutions have become imperative. This chapter offers insights into how IoT-enabled devices, coupled with AI, transform parking management systems, improving urban traffic flow and enhancing user convenience.

The third chapter, *Fusion of Blockchain and Machine Learning: A Case of Secure Smart Grid*, highlights the synergy between two revolutionary technologies—blockchain and machine learning. Addressing the critical need for secure and efficient energy systems, this chapter explores how their integration can create robust, decentralised smart grids. The discussion provides a forward-thinking perspective on managing energy resources while ensuring transparency and security.

IoT's potential in education takes centre stage in the fourth chapter, Perspective Chapter: *Unlocking the Potential of IoT in Education – Overcoming the Obstacles to Integration in Spanish Universities Using the Ishikawa Diagram*. This chapter systematically examines the barriers hindering IoT adoption in academic institutions and employs the Ishikawa Diagram to offer structured solutions. Doing so emphasises IoT's transformative potential to enrich educational experiences and foster innovation.

The fifth chapter, *Perspective Chapter: The Evolution of Edge Computing in the IoT Era of the Twenty-Second Century*, provides a visionary analysis of edge computing's role in shaping IoT's future. As IoT devices proliferate, decentralised data processing at the edge becomes vital for efficiency and scalability. This chapter explores the challenges and opportunities of implementing edge computing, envisioning its role in the 22nd-century technological ecosystem.

Finally, the sixth chapter, *Perspective Chapter: Is IoMT EHR Integration Leading to Better Patient Health and Well-Being*, investigates the transformative impact of integrating the Internet of Medical Things (IoMT) with electronic health records (EHR). This chapter critically analyses how this integration influences patient outcomes and health system efficiency. Addressing both the potential benefits and challenges offers a balanced perspective on IoT's role in healthcare innovation.

This edited volume represents the collective effort of numerous contributors who have shared their expertise to provide an insightful overview of IoT's evolution and applications. We extend our heartfelt gratitude to the authors, reviewers, and academic community members whose dedication made this volume possible. Special thanks are due to the editorial team and assistants whose work ensured the seamless curation of this book.

We hope this volume will inspire researchers, practitioners, and policymakers to explore the transformative potential of IoT further. The discussions presented herein serve as both a reflection of current advancements and a beacon for future innovations in navigating the Internet of Things in the 22nd century.

Muhammad Usman Tariq
Abu Dhabi University,
Abu Dhabi, UAE

Section 1

AI and Machine Learning

Chapter 1

From Sensors to Smart Decisions: Building an Intelligent Irrigation System with Machine Learning

Samuel Zeyede Tefera and Asrat Mulatu Beyene

Abstract

An intelligent irrigation system, powered by Machine Learning (ML) and Internet of Things (IoT), can significantly optimize water usage and enhance crop production. This research proposes such a system, using IoT devices to collect real-time soil and environmental data. ML algorithms analyze these data to provide real-time irrigation recommendations. Simulation and prototype testing demonstrated the system's effectiveness in minimizing water consumption. For garlic, Crop Water Requirement (CWR) was reduced by 6.45% and 6.72% during initial and development stages. Additionally, the system can predict optimal crop types. Future work with longer-term data and more evaluation parameters could further refine the system's insights.

Keywords: agricultural automation, internet of things based systems, machine learning techniques, prototype implementation, simulation modeling, smart and intelligent irrigation systems

1. Introduction

Agriculture, without a doubt, has the potential to contribute to industrialization by providing raw materials for industries, bringing foreign exchange to the country, and securing food on the plate for families. That is particularly true for developing countries like Ethiopia where agriculture is the livelihood of the majority [1]. Ethiopia's economy is mostly centered on subsistence agriculture, which contributes 50% of the country's GDP and employs approximately 85% of the workforce. According to the World Bank [2], in 2018 Ethiopia has around 16.187 million hectares of arable land with a wide range of weather possibilities. By 2050, the world's population is predicted to reach about 10 billion people. That is 3.4 billion extra mouths to feed. Besides, global food demand is expected to rise as high as by 98%. This necessitates that agriculture must improve the production and yields of products [3]. This demands the use of technological solutions to optimize agricultural resource usage. At places where agricultural production merely depends on seasonal rainfall, like Ethiopia, it has become increasingly erratic and unreliable due to global climate change and man-made causes [1, 4]. Rapid developments in crop production technologies are required to keep up with the steady rise in food consumption. In developing countries, food insecurity is a big issue. In Ethiopia, where the economy is mostly built on agriculture, the use of technology to increase yields is a major requirement [5].

Irrigation systems have been under pressure to produce more with lower supplies of water. Various innovative practices can bring economic advantages while reducing environmental burdens such as water abstraction, energy use, pollutants, among others by using technology [6, 7].

Therefore, in this work, recent advancements in IoTs and ML algorithms are used to use historical and real-time weather data to predict the need of water and fertilizers and control the same remotely. Here, relevant works since 2017 are collected on notable research databases, see **Table 1**, using keywords like "smart irrigation", "intelligent irrigation", "IoT based irrigation system", "ML based irrigation system", and "smart and intelligent irrigation system".

As can be seen in **Table 2**, the main research gaps identified includes but not limited to: Though some works tried to use ML techniques and sensors they only worked on data collection and prediction. There is no decision making or classification. Moreover, none worked on a remotely accessible platform to make decision like watering. It is also rare to find a simulation study of a smart and intelligent agriculture system backed by a prototype implementation.

The majority of irrigation systems in Ethiopia are operated manually [17, 18]. The following are the most serious agricultural problems during crop production both locally and globally based on [12] nutrient imbalance, water-logging, acidification, contamination, erosion, salinization; water wastage related to drainage, outflow, inflow, and evaporation. Crop yields are reduced due to non-uniform availability of moisture. The amount of labor used in manual irrigation system is higher.

These points show that monitoring the level of nutrients, water, moisture, labor, and contextual knowledge are very critical in the administration of a successful agricultural system. However, it is time for technologies to takeover such activities by automating with less resources to extract knowledge helping better decision making. Hence, in this research work, the primary aim is to use ML algorithms to design a

Research database	Search string used	Date accessed	Filter applied	Result	Remark
IEEE Xplore	Smart irrigation	April–May 2022	Conference Proceedings	90	25 are applicable
Science Direct	Smart, IoT & ML in irrigation system	April–May 2022	Journals	65	18 are applicable
Scopus	Smart, IoT & ML in irrigation system	April–May 2022	Journals and Conference Proceedings	35	10 are applicable
Web of Science	Smart irrigation systems	April–May 2022	Journals	20	3 are applicable

Table 1.
Summary of research databases where articles are retrieved.

Author	Technology used			Features implemented	
	Central controller	**IoTs or sensors**	**AI or/and ML algorithm**	**Data collected**	**Monitoring & controlling**
[8]	Raspberry pi and Arduino	Rain and soil Moisture sensor	Neural network	Soil moisture and rain	Predict the future of soil moisture.
[9]	Raspberry pi	Soil moisture, Humidity, and temperature	No	Humidity, temperature, and Soil moisture	Management of Water
[10]	RFID PCA	pH and Temperature sensors	Linear regression and decision tree	Soil nutrient level, temperature of atmosphere	Soil Nutrient Degradation Level.
[11]	NodeMCU	Soil Moisture, pH sensor, and PIR sensor	No	Soil moisture and pH of the soil	Watering the field based on the threshold value.
[12]	ZigBee	Soil moisture, Temperature, and Water level	K-means clustering algorithm	System analyses weather reports.	Control pests Weather forecasting
[13]	ZigBee Raspberry Pi	Soil moisture and Humidity sensor	Random Forest	Soil moisture Nutrient	Crop management Nutrient Detection
[14]	LoRa technology	Water level sensor	No	Optimal time irrigate and amount of water	Management of Water.
[15]	Wi-Fi Raspberry Pi	Temperature, soil moisture, and light sensor	MQTT protocol	Humidity, temperature, soil moisture and light intensity	Weather monitoring and precision farming.
[16]	ESP32	Temperature, soil moisture, Ultrasonic Distance Sensor	MQTT protocol	Temperature, moisture and distance	Irrigation control and optimum water utilization.

MQTT - Message Queuing Telemetry Transport; RFID – Radio Frequency Identification; PCA - Principal Component Analysis; LoRa - Long Range Radio; PIR - Passive InfraRed.

Table 2.
Technologies used in recent related works.

model based on historical data and use IoTs to collect real-time data to monitor and control agricultural fields at any given time remotely. This is expected to improve water usage, nutrient imbalance, among others with less human intervention.

2. Materials and methods

In this research work, both simulation study and prototype implementation are used. A simplified version of the methodology used in this work is depicted in **Figure 1**.

2.1 Description of the study area

The historical data collection and field experiment are conducted at the Debre Zeit Agricultural Research Center (DZARC) which is found in the Oromia Regional State in East Shoa Zone. As shown in **Figure 1**, Debre Zeit is a small town located around 42 kilometers in the eastern side of the Capital city, Addis Ababa. The area receives an annual mean rainfall of roughly 810.3 mm, with a bimodal trend and medium yearly variability [17].

In Ethiopia, seasonal fluctuations and atmospheric pressure systems create four distinct seasons: Kiremt/Meher or summer (June to August), Tsedey or spring (September to November), Bega or winter (December to February), Belg or autumn (March to May) [19, 20]. About 76% of the area's total rainfall is in the Kiremt or rainy season, 15% in Belg, and the rest in the Bega or dry season, which necessitates irrigation [19, 20].

2.2 Data collection

In this research work, data has been collected using both primary and secondary sources.

Primary data: The primary data is collected from different field sensors so that the instantaneous environmental data of soil moisture, temperature, pH, and Rain are captured well. The MH Sensor Series for soil moisture, the LM35 sensor series for temperature, pH meter v.1.1, and YL-83 for rain are used to collect the respective primary data from the research area sized 1 m^2. The data has been collected for three consecutive months from November and December 2021 to January of 2022. The total size of the data was 1657 rows by 4 columns being the latter representing rainfall, temperature, pH, and moisture.

Secondary data: The secondary data used in this work are obtained from the DZARC. The data collection techniques used include document analysis like archives & reports, field visits, and face-to-face interviews with agronomists, & researchers.

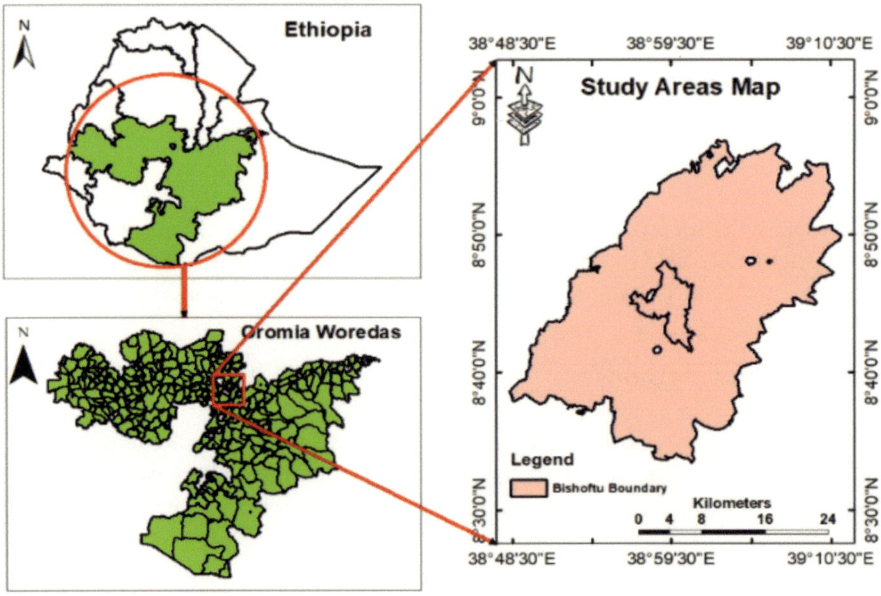

Figure 1.
Map of the study area.

Moreover, desk research has been used extensively to access published documents relevant to the research topic and research area. The overall data collected contains 10-year weather data that contains, among others, rain, humidity, temperature, and moisture.

In **Figure 2**, we have shown the data preprocessing steps adopted in this work.

2.3 Simulation modeling and analysis of results

Simulation modeling and analysis have been conducted using Proteus 8.10 Professional, python, ThingSpeak and MATLAB. Proteus is used to design and simulate the proposed system. Python is used to write the different features of the simulation, and ThingSpeak is IoT-based cloud platform that stores and analyzes the various data collected, and finally, displays the overall result. It uses MATLAB for data analysis and presentation.

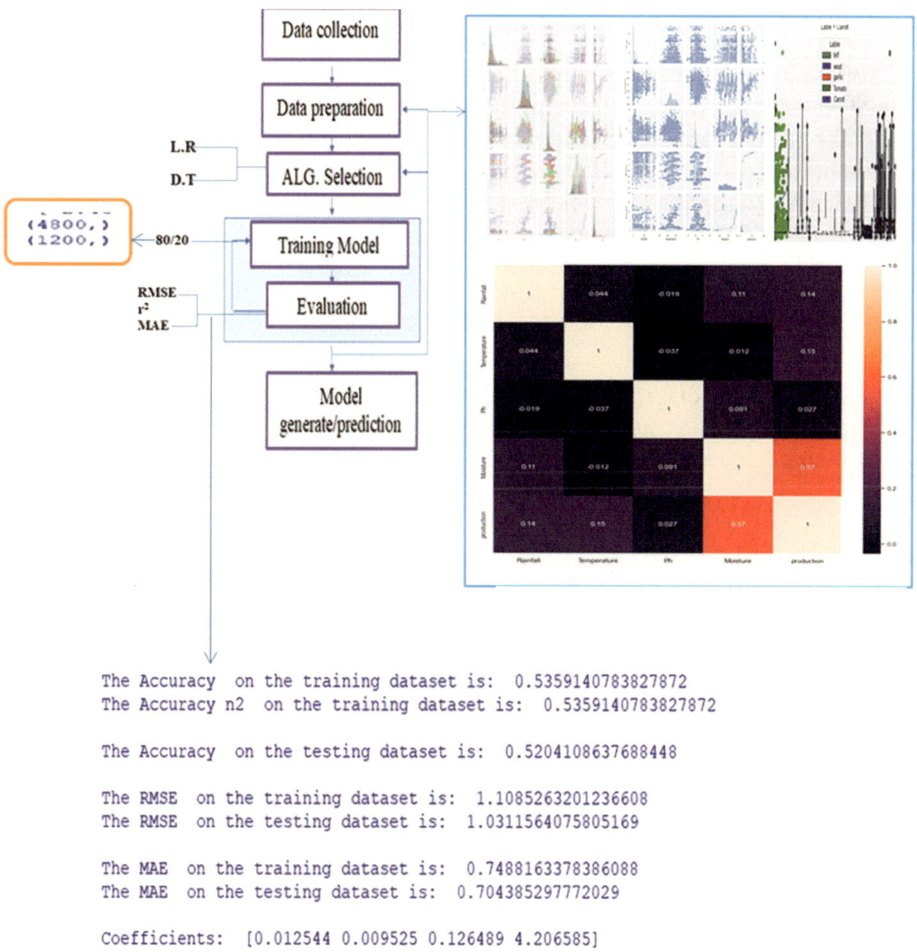

Figure 2.
Data preprocessing steps.

2.4 Prototype implementation and analysis

During the prototype implementation, Raspberry Pi 3 is used as the central controller, four sensors to monitor moisture, temperature, pH, and Rain, and various modules like the GSM module to send data to the user/farmer, display module for local visualization, analog to digital converter (ADC1115), motor drive are used.

2.5 Comparative analysis of results

Finally, both the results obtained from simulation and prototype implementations are comparatively analyzed against the state-of-the-art to showcase the contributions made and open issues to be workout in the future.

3. Results

3.1 The proposed smart and intelligent irrigation system (SI2S)

This research work proposes IoT-enabled and ML-trained irrigation system for optimal water usage with the least human intervention. In the agriculture field, IoT sensors are used to capture instantaneous soil and environmental data. The collected data is sent to and stored in a cloud server, which uses ML algorithms to analyze and make irrigation/watering and soil nutrient recommendations to the farmer. In light of this, a smart and intelligent irrigation system with a lower total cost of ownership that can be used for various application scenarios is developed.

3.2 System architecture

The system block diagram of the proposed solution is shown in **Figure 3**. It shows the three main components of the proposed system. First is IoT sensors, which collect environmental data like soil moisture, temperature, pH, and rain. The second is

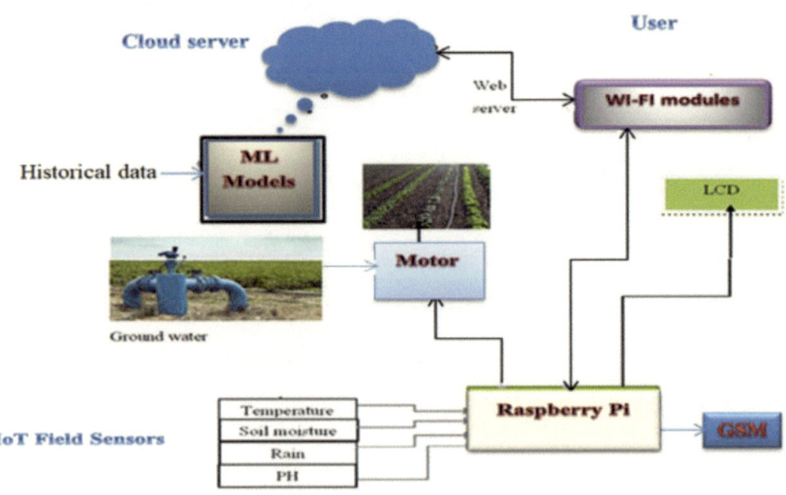

Figure 3.
Proposed system architecture.

microcontroller module, which integrates and analyzes the real-time data collected from the various sensors with the historical data maintained in the cloud to make various decisions. The third is cloud System, which maintains the historical data and the data collected from various sensors. The ML model is maintained in Google Cloud server that enables further communication with the user/farmer.

3.3 Simulation modeling and implementation

We employed two different ML algorithms for prediction and classification purposes. In smart agriculture research, linear regression and decision tree are the most commonly used algorithms for prediction and classification, respectively [13, 21–24].

3.4 Prediction algorithms used

In our work, linear regression is used for prediction based on the recommendations of the aforementioned researchers. The researchers claimed, among the various ML algorithms, linear regression is preferable for agricultural systems. In our work, this model is used to figure out how crop production will change based on past historical data and current field sensor data. It is used to recommend whether irrigation and nutrients are necessary, or not. The equation that describes the linear regression model based on Yimam et al. [20] model is presented in **Figure 4.**

In this work, the above equation is contextualized as shown in Eq. (1).

$$Y = \alpha + \beta 1^{*} \text{ rainfall} + \beta 2^{*} \text{ soil moister} + \beta 3^{*} \ pH + \beta 3^{*} \text{ temperature} + e. \quad (1)$$

3.5 Classification algorithm used

Decision trees are designed to mirror human thinking abilities when making decisions [25]. In this work, the decision tree algorithm depicted in **Figure 5** is used to classify the historical weather data of the research area. The same recommendation as the prediction algorithms was used as selection criteria based on Abioye et al. [13], Jahanavi and Sushma [21]; Klompenburg et al. [24]; Rashid et al. [22]; and Rayhana et al. [23].

3.6 Schematics of the simulation implementation

The proposed system simulation model is implemented using Proteus as presented in **Figure 6**. It contains a Raspberry Pi 3 microcontroller, four sensors, and other devices.

$$Y = a + \beta 1\, X1 + \beta 2\, X2 + \ldots + \beta n\, Xn + e$$

Where:

Y = either a dependent or a response variable.
X = denotes a predictor or independent variable.
α = an abbreviation for 'constant'.
β = estimated coefficient or slope.
e = is the error.

Figure 4.
Linear regression model used in this work.

Step 1: Start with the root node, which holds the entire dataset.

Step 2: Using the Attribute Selection Measure (ASM), find the best attribute in the dataset.

Step 3: Subdivide the data into subsets that contain the best value the given attribute.

Step 4: Create the node of the decision tree that has the best attribute value.

Step 5: Create additional decision trees in a recursive manner using the subsets of the dataset obtained in step 3.

Continue this process until the nodes can no longer be classified, at which point the final node is designated as a leaf node.

Figure 5.
Decision tree algorithm used.

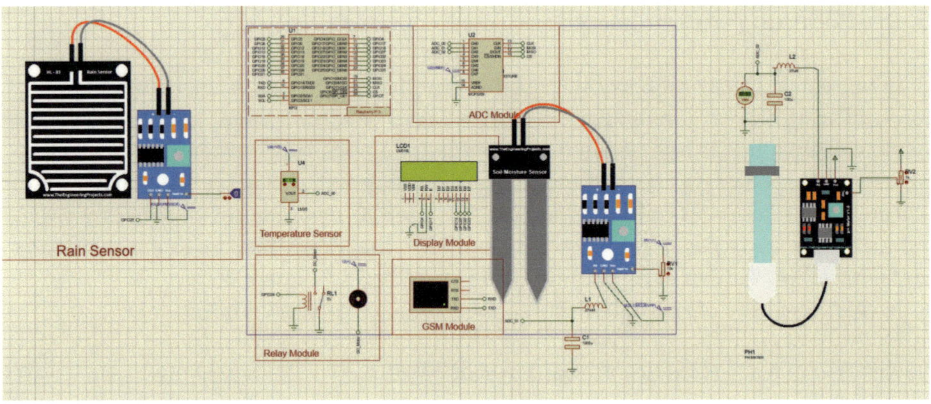

Figure 6.
Proteus simulation design schematic diagram.

Temperature, pH, moisture, and rain sensors are used in this system to monitor the existing weather conditions of the agricultural area. A relay module triggers the water pump motors, while the GSM module sends messages to the user's phone, the LCD panel displays field data, and the analog-to-digital converter (ADC) transforms analog signals to digital for the Raspberry Pi. The ADC is needed since the Raspberry Pi has only digital general-purpose input–output (GPIO) pins whereas the moisture, pH, and temperature sensors generate analog outputs. The Wi-Fi module connects the ThingSpeak cloud to the Raspberry Pi.

The Raspberry Pi sends data harvested from the four sensors to the cloud, and then, analyzes and stores it on the ThingSpeak server. Additionally, the data is shown in real time on the ThingSpeak Dashboard.

3.7 Flowchart of the overall implementation

When the ML algorithm and the field sensor data meet the threshold value, the water pump will switch on to efficiently irrigate the plant until it reaches the specified value.

When the pH value is between 5.5 and 7.5, without inclusion, the soil has enough nutrients. Otherwise, the soil is deficient in nutrients and minerals.

The flowchart in **Figure 7** shows the steps the proposed system goes through in monitoring the agricultural field using sensors, push the data to the cloud whenever Wi-Fi is available, use the ML algorithms to predict whether irrigation and/or

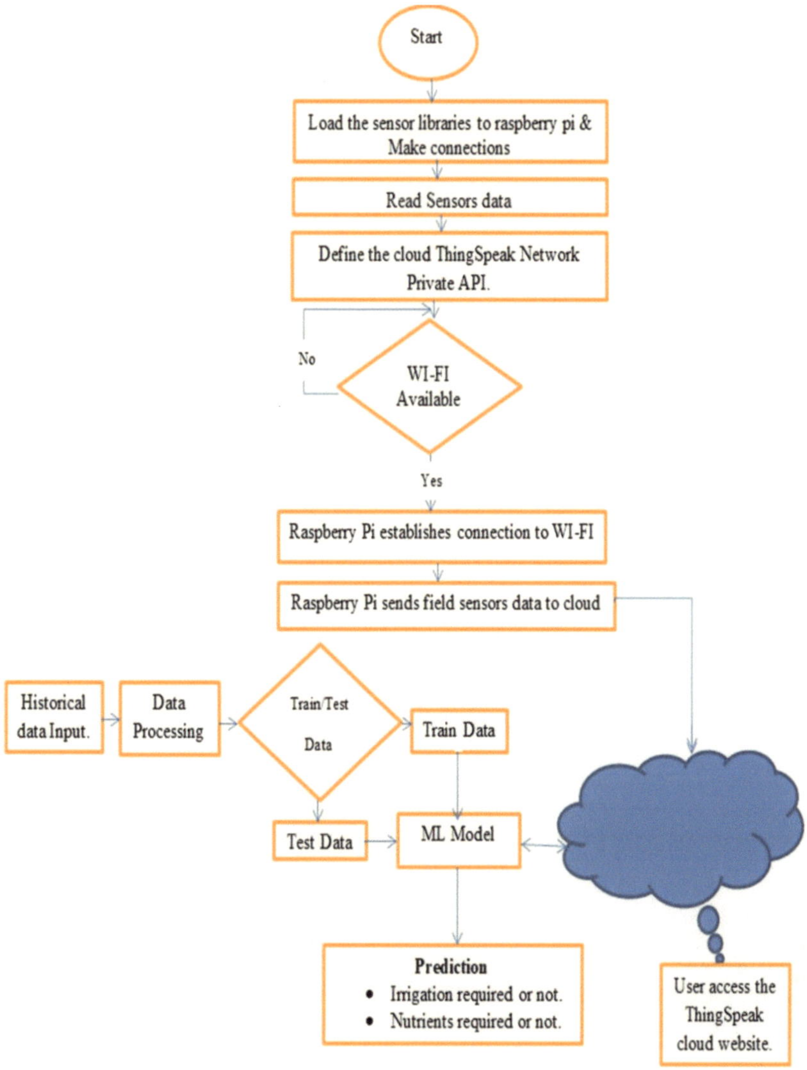

Figure 7.
Flow chart of the overall implementation.

nutrients are required, and notify the same to the user. Besides, whenever the user receives that the agricultural field needs irrigation it is possible to trigger the relay to initiate the water pump to irrigate the crops.

3.8 Analysis of simulation results

3.8.1 ThingSpeak IoT simulation results

The expected result of the simulation is that all sensors are properly connected and configured to communicate with the Raspberry Pi using Python programs. Then data is sent to the cloud server via Wi-Fi connection. Finally, the real-time data is displayed on the ThingSpeak cloud server platform as shown in **Figure 8**.

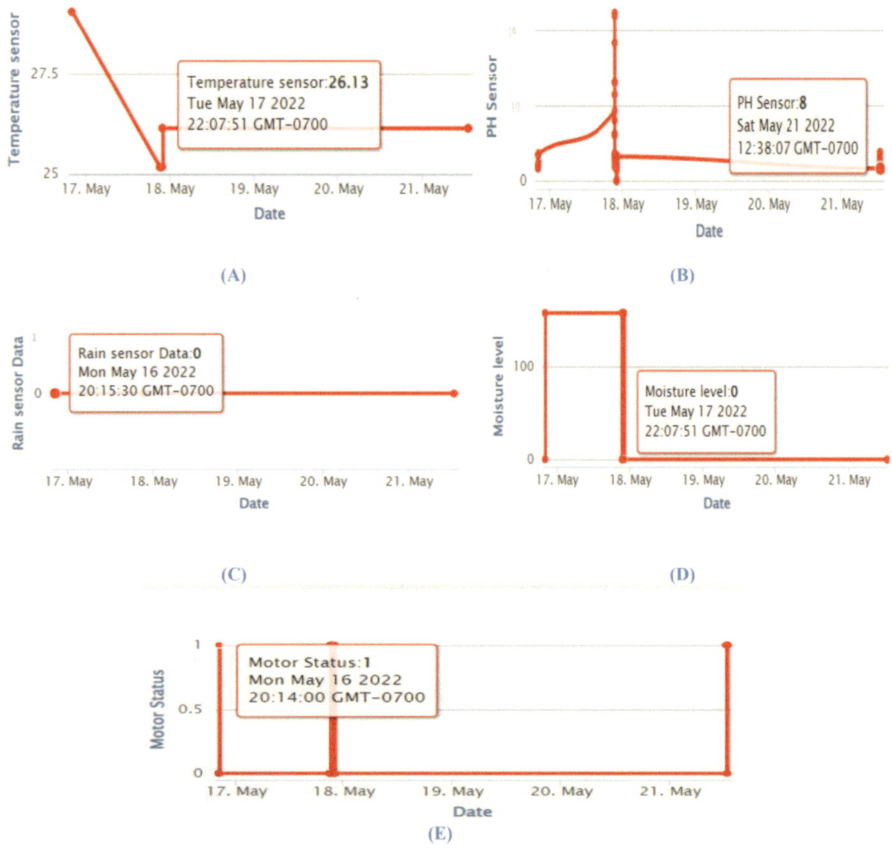

Figure 8.
Real-time data from field sensors. (A) Temperature, (B) pH, (C) Rain, (D) Moisture, and (E) Motor.

Using the Cloud web server of the ThingSpeak application, one can remotely monitor the data from anywhere. As seen in **Figure 8**, it is possible to monitor the field sensors of rain, soil moisture, pH, and temperature as well as the status of the relay.

3.8.2 Production model result

This model is used to figure out how crop production and field data characteristics are related. This model assists in estimating the amount of production of crops. To determine the link between production and each of the four parameters (soil moisture, temperature, pH and rain), we use linear regression. **Figure 9** shows the production rate with the four parameters.

Figure 10 presents the real-time agricultural field data collected from the four sensors. It also shows the recommendation of irrigating the field based on both historical and real-time weather data. Since the system recommends that irrigation is required the user enabled the relay motor to pump water and irrigate the field, and hence, the motor status is on. The system automatically switches the motor off when the moisture sensor passes the threshold value or rain falls where both are detected by the sensors.

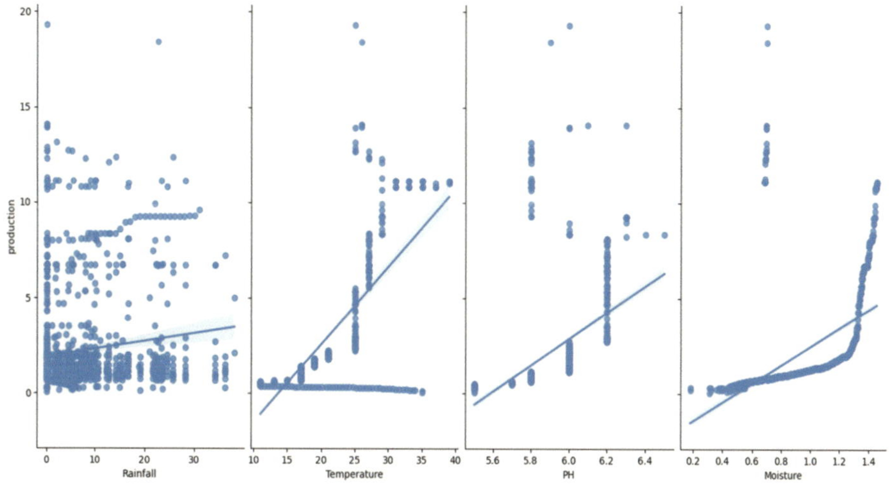

Figure 9.
Production predicted model.

```
['28.06', '0', '1']
Temperature:  28.06
Moisture of the soil is:  0
Motor status:  1
rain:  0
Irrigation is required
Root Mean Square error is:  1.7032768222093186
```

Figure 10.
Information generated based on historical and real-time data.

3.8.3 pH value prediction result

Soil pH, often known as soil response, is a measurement of the acidity or alkalinity of soil. The pH scale ranges from 0 to 14, with pH 7 representing neutrality.

The pH of the soil lowers as the amount of hydrogen ions in the soil rises, making it more acidic. The soil becomes more acidic from pH 7 to 0, and more alkaline or basic from pH 7 to 14 [9].

Soil pH indicates whether or not crops need nutrients to keep the appropriate pH balance. **Figure 11** presets typical crops and their pH values.

As seen in **Figure 12**, the pH value of the soil is zero. This alerts the user that the soil is becoming increasingly acidic with fertilizer and mineral deficiencies. Based on the specific type of crop, appropriate acid treatment could be made by applying the right fertilizers.

As shown in **Figure 13**, the system can also predict and suggest crop types that could provide better production based on historical data.

3.9 Prototyping of the smart and intelligent irrigation system (SI2S)

A prototype implementation using low-cost field sensors interfaced with a Raspberry Pi microcontroller has been made to design a smart and intelligent irrigation monitoring and control system.

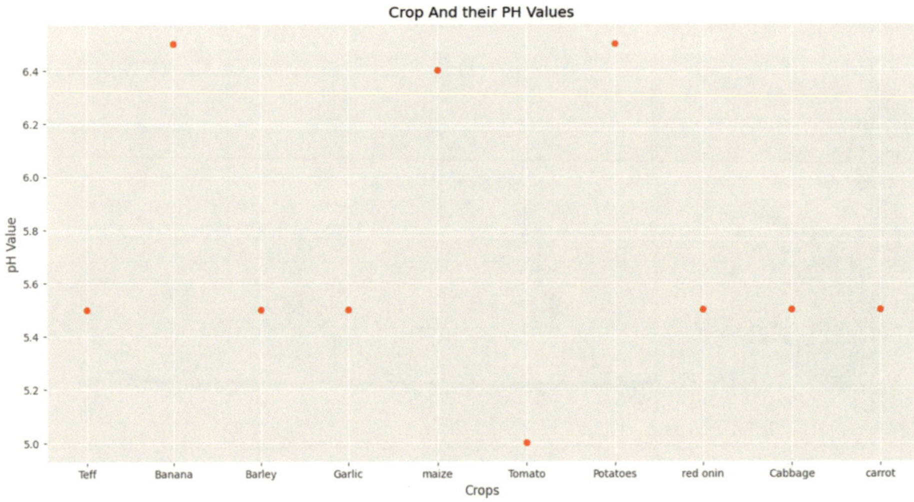

Figure 11.
pH Value prediction model result.

```
H1.py
Coefficients:
 [ 2.43293158e-17 -2.01227923e-16  1.23859256e-15  1.00000000e+00]
Variance score: 1.00000
Mean squared error: 0.00000
['28.06', '314', '0']
pH of the soil is:  0
The soil is deficient of nutrients and minerals
```

Figure 12.
pH Data generated to indicate current soil condition.

```
>>>
==== RESTART: C:\Users\samiok\Desktop\MOCK DOC FOR DR,AST
 FOR DEPARTEMENT\ML Codes and datasets\crop predection\cr
.py ===
The accuracy of this model is:   99.35483870967742
['29.03', '157', '0']
pH of the soil is:  7
The soil has enough nutrients
The predicted crop is barley
>>>
= RESTART: C:\Users\samiok\Desktop\MOCK DOC FOR DR,AST\FI
R DEPARTEMENT\ML Codes and datasets\crop predection\crop_
The accuracy of this model is:   99.46236559139786
['29.03', '157', '0']
pH of the soil is:  10
The soil is deficient of nutrients but has minerals
The predicted crop is barley
>>>

= RESTART: C:\Users\samiok\Desktop\MOCK DOC FOR DR,AST\FIN
R DEPARTEMENT\ML Codes and datasets\crop predection\crop_p
The accuracy of this model is:   99.13978494623656
['29.03', '157', '0']
pH of the soil is:  11
The soil is deficient of nutrients but has minerals
The predicted crop is Garlic
```

Figure 13.
Crop prediction result.

3.10 Prototype model and components

The proposed prototype is designed and developed using a variety of hardware, software, and platforms. The experimental setup with the main hardware components and their interconnections and interfacing with the microcontroller are depicted in **Figure 14**.

Moisture, pH, rain, temperature, and humidity Sensors were put in the field. Once the soil reaches the desired moisture, temperature, and pH level, the sensors send a signal to the Raspberry Pi to control and send field data information to the cloud server. The ML model in the cloud processes the real-time data based on the model developed from the historical data. Users can view, monitor, and control data in the ThingSpeak cloud server web application ubiquitously.

3.11 Weather data collection using the prototype system

The DZARC provided the historical weather data that is used in this study. During the prototype implementation, garlic was chosen since it is already well cultivated in the center with adequate historical data for the proposed system to compare with. For Garlic, the cumulative reference evapotranspiration (ET 0) in the research center was 77.5 mm for the initial stage and 136.7 mm for the development phase of net crop water demand, as indicated in **Table 3** and **Figure 13**. The cumulative reference evapotranspiration (ET 0) was 72.5 mm for the starting stage and 127.7 mm for the development stage for the interval between planting and the beginning of the irrigation experiment, which has a month difference. This is depicted in **Figure 15**.

The proposed system water usage when compared with the research center practice is displayed in **Table 4** and **Figure 16**. The highest water demand was reported during the development stage for both in the proposed system and in the research center practice. However, the proposed system utilized lesser CRW of 6.45 and 6.72% amount of water during the initial and development stages, respectively.

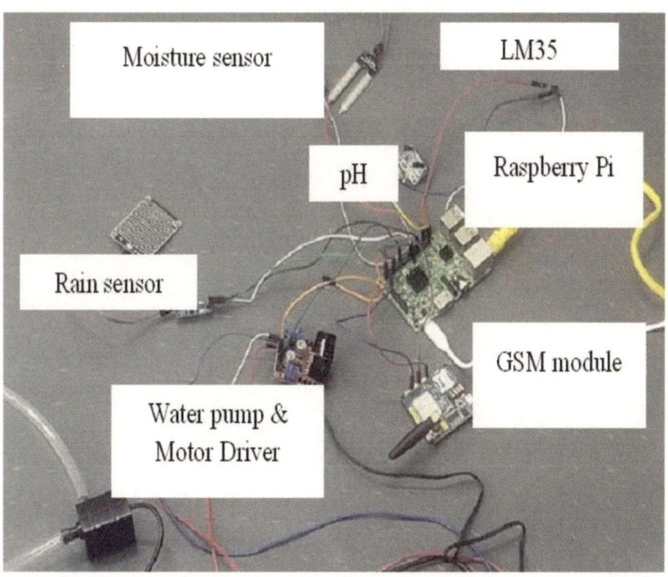

Figure 14.
Prototype implementation of the proposed irrigation system.

Month	Decade	Stage	Kc	ET 0 mm/ day	ET 0 mm/ dec	Rain mm/dec	IR mm/ dec	Stage CWR
Nov.	1	Initial	0.7	2.05	20.5	0.1	20.4	
Nov.	2	Initial	0.7	2.86	28.6	0	28.6	
Nov.	3	Initial	0.7	2.84	28.4	0	28.4	77.5
Dec.	1	Devt sg.	0.72	2.9	29	0	29	
Dec.	2	Devt sg.	0.8	3.17	31.7	0	31.7	
Dec.	3	Devt sg.	0.88	3.48	34.8	0	34.8	
Jan.	1	Devt sg.	0.96	3.79	37.9	0	37.9	136.9

NB: CWR (mm) stands for Crop Water Requirement in millimeters, Kc for Crop Coefficient, IR for Irrigation Requirement, and ET 0 for Crop Evapotranspiration, Devt sg. = Development Stage, RCP = Research Centre Practice, PS = Proposed Smart Intelligent Irrigation System (SI^2S).

Table 3.
Water demand for garlic at research center practice (RCP).

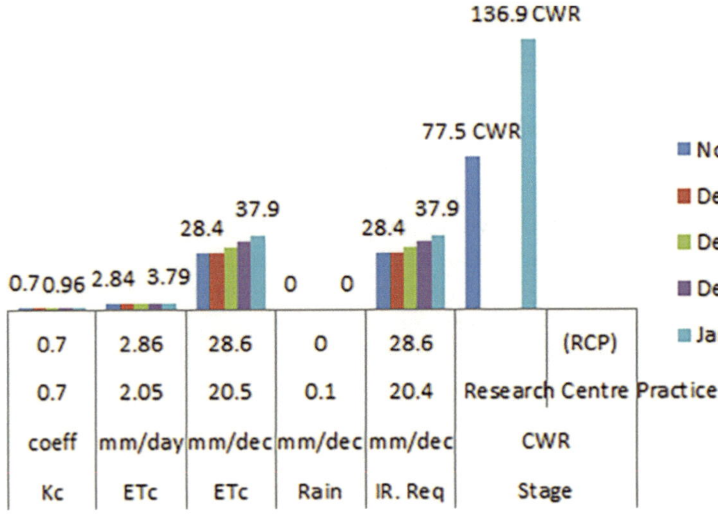

Figure 15.
RCP water demand of Garlic.

Month	Decade	Stage	Kc	ET 0 mm/ day	ET 0 mm/ dec	Rain mm/ dec	IR mm/ dec	Stage CWR
Nov.	1	Initial	0.7	2. 02	20.2	0	20.2	
Nov.	2	Initial	0.7	2.64	26.4	0	26.4	
Nov.	3	Initial	0.7	2.54	25.4	0	25.4	72.5
Dec.	1	Devt sg.	0.72	2.67	26.7	0	26.7	
Dec.	2	Devt sg.	0.8	3.01	30.1	0	30.1	
Dec.	3	Devt sg.	0.88	3.45	34.5	0.1	34.4	
Jan.	1	Devt sg.	0.96	3.65	36.5	0	36.5	127.7

NB: Decade (or dec) means 1/10th

Table 4.
Water demand for Garlic in the proposed system.

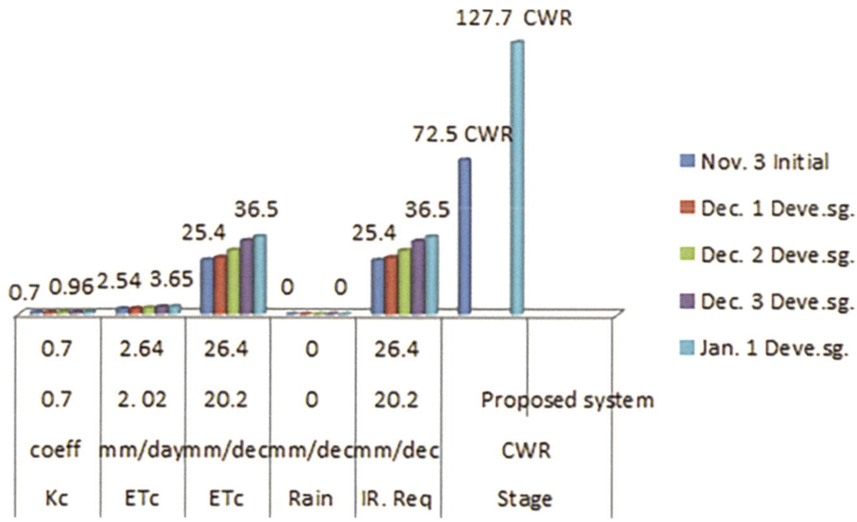

Figure 16.
Water demand for Garlic in the proposed system.

4. Discussion

When the proposed SI^{2}S compared with traditional irrigation systems, it is more intelligent in that it chooses when to irrigate the plant based on real-time data from IoT-based field sensors. Moreover, it uses ML-based prediction and classification models to achieve better resource utilization with minimum physical intervention. The prediction model, which is based on linear regression model, analyzes both historical weather data and real-time sensor data to recommend whether irrigation is required at that specific time. The classification model uses decision tree to recommend the type crop to plant this season. This is also done using historical weather data and current soil data collected from the IoT sensors. These approaches not only save lots of time it improves resource utilization like water and nutrients. The water demand of the crop can be monitored via the moisture, temperature, and rain sensors whereas; the level of soil nutrients is monitored based on pH sensor. In traditional irrigation systems, there is a waste of resources such as water, nutrients, labor, and time [1, 6, 26]. To justify this, the proposed SI^{2}S is compared with traditional irrigation systems, and with selected and appropriate smart irrigation systems previously proposed with detailed analysis, in **Tables 5–7**. More specifically, based on the results shown in **Tables 3** and **4** the proposed system improved the CWR of Initial and Development stages of the selected crop during the prototype study, which is Garlic, by 6.45 and 6.72%, respectively.

As can be seen in **Table 5**, traditional systems lack much of the means to utilize agricultural resources including labor, time, water, and fertilizers, among others when compared to the proposed system. Primarily, that is why emerging technologies need to be adapted to such application domains [12, 17]. Obviously, the proposed system performed better in almost all aspects when compared with traditional systems. Apparently, that is something expected. Hence, **Tables 6** and 7 compared the proposed system with similar systems to get a more critical and realistic performance comparison with related works that identified as smart and intelligent [8, 23, 30, 33].

Table 6 shows selected related works that are similar to the proposed work where many lack the automatic control of the agricultural field using actuators or motors to

Performance indicator	Traditional irrigation methods	The proposed SI^2S
Water saving	A lot of water is wasted [18, 20]. Drainage, outflow, and evaporation cause losses [18, 27]	Water can be saved. The losses from runoff and deep percolation are minimal or negligible.
Labor saving	The amount of labor used in each round of irrigation is higher [6, 28]	Labor is required only for initial setup and occasional maintenance.
Weed infestation	Is very high [13, 29]	Weed infestation is very low or non-existent due to minimal soil moisture.
Use of saline water	The concentration of salts rises, posing a danger to plant growth [1]	The salt concentration in the root zone is kept below dangerous levels by frequent irrigation.
Problems with diseases and pests	High [30]	Because of the regulated atmospheric humidity, it is relatively less.
Suitability in a variety of soils	Deep percolation is more common in light soils and at shallow depths. Heavy soils lose more runoff.	Because the flow rate can be regulated, it is suitable for all soil types.
Water management	Very difficult to manage the water [31]	Easily & efficiently managed.
Fertilizer use efficiency	Because to high losses owing to leaching and runoff, the level is low [29]	Very high due to reduced loss of nutrients through leaching and runoff.
Soil erosion	High [1, 29–31]	Due to partial wetting of the soil surface and sluggish application rates, less is produced.
Increasing crop yields	Crop yields are reduced due to non-uniform availability of moisture [1, 29–31]	Crop yields increase because of uniform moisture availability
Water and resource optimization	Very low because it does not have any mechanism to control the water and the other resources it uses only by observation in the field [29–32]	Highly optimize the water and the resource because it decides intelligently for irrigating the plant

Table 5.
Comparative performance analysis of traditional irrigation systems with the proposed SI2S.

Author	IoT-based solution	Field data collected	IoT monitoring capability
[30]	Use sensors for detection.	Temperature and humidity	Management of water
[33]	Data collection and immediate notification is sent to farmers.	Soil moisture and temperature	Management of Water
[23]	Farmers can know field status.	Soil moisture, temperature & Humidity.	Management of Water
[24]	Enhanced crop yield by proper water management.	Temperature, Humidity, Soil moisture, Rainfall, and Soil pH.	Production and Water Management
[34]	Crop-field monitoring and irrigation automation system	Soil moisture and temperature	Crop development with the least amount of water accessible to the plants.
Proposed System	Automatically irrigate without human intervention based on field sensors and historical data based ML model.	Soil moisture, Temp, Rain, pH value simulated	It is possible to regulate water, fertilizers, and minerals as well as predict crop type.

Table 6.
Comparative summary of related works against the proposed system.

DOI: http://dx.doi.org/10.5772/intechopen.1006379

Author	Features			Performance		Method of Analysis	
	Smart		Intelligent (ML model)	Water Optimization	TCO	Simulation	Prototype
[33]	Irrigation automation system and Crop-field monitoring.	Smart	No	Good	Medium	No	Yes
[33]	Mechanism to control humidity and temperature.				Low	No	Yes
[23]	Model for measuring and recording the growth level of plants in a greenhouse.				Low	No	No
	A ML technique is applied to optimize water usage in irrigation by predicting future soil moisture.		Yes, predicts soil moisture only.	Better	Medium	Yes	Yes
Proposed System (SI^{2}S)	ML algorithms are used to design a model based on historical data IoTs are used to collect real-time data to monitor and control agricultural fields at any given time remotely ML model make prediction based on historical and real-time data Notifies the user and makes self-decisions		Yes, predicts both irrigation and nutrient requirements.	Better	Low	Yes	Yes

NB. TCO, Total Cost of Ownership, is calculated as Initial Cost + Maintenance Cost – Remaining Cost. The Initial Cost includes material purchase and design expenses, Maintenance Cost covers running costs like preventive maintenance and support. The Remaining Cost is a deduction of devaluation values from the previous two. Based on a calculation made using this formula we assessed works closely related to ours. This gives us a range of TCO values that can be categorized as low below 1000 USD, medium those ranging between 1000 & 3000 USD, and high above 3000 USD. Accordingly, the proposed work and other related works are evaluated and the result is populated in this table. Available from: https://rockcontent.com/blog/total-cost-of-ownership/

Table 7.
Comparative performance analysis of the proposed system against previous works.

initiate irrigation, for example. In the proposed system, the farmer or user can monitor the agricultural field anywhere in the world via the online system through their smartphone. While doing so she can initiate irrigating the plants based on the sensor data that indicated the need for water. Moreover, none attempted to use ML algorithms to create an AI model that can predict the type of crop that better be planted in the area.

When it comes to **Table 7**, a detailed performance comparison is made between the proposed SI^2S system and the selected related works that are claimed smart and intelligent. The proposed model is better in some critical aspects like the use of both simulation analysis and prototype implementation. The prototype implementation is made using low-cost hardware where it is possible to replicate the work for real-world implementations by low-income farmers both in rural and urban settings. As long as electric power is made available through commercial lines or batteries backed by, for example, renewable energy sources, then it is possible to deploy it in any setting to monitor and control a farming area of crops, vegetables, horticulture, and fruits.

5. Conclusions, contributions and future works

5.1 Conclusions

In conclusion, this work discusses a smart and intelligent irrigation system (SI^2S). It is smart because the proposed model has four sensors that monitor moisture, pH, rain, and temperature of the soil. And, it is intelligent because it has ML models built using a 10-year historical data of DZARC where the prototype was deployed for 3 months. The classification model, which is based on a decision tree algorithm, categorizes the type of crop that could better be planted. This model, though trained and tested using the historical data uses the real-time sensor data to further fine tune its classification. The prediction model, which is based on the linear regression algorithm, suggests the need for water/irrigation and nutrients of the soil based on both historical and instantaneous weather data.

Though there are many possible extensions, this system has improved the CWR of garlic at its initial and development stages when compared with previous works. Moreover, it can be used to get suggestions about which crop could be better planted in the current season to get better production based on the historical and real-time data of soil pH and other parameters. Farmers and agriculturalists can remotely monitor their fields using a computer or mobile device via the cloud-based web application. The data collected through the sensors which is saved in the cloud could be used for further research and analysis in numerous ways to improve production.

By doing so, this system avoids physical presence, saves time, and improves water usage, among other things. Installation is simple, and the amount of labor and time required to control the irrigation process is minimal. Better performances and features are observed from the system when compared with similar recent works.

5.2 Contributions

The following are the main contributions of this study: First, the proposed system minimized the Crop Water Requirement (CWR) of Garlic by 6.45 and 6.72% during its Initial and Development stages, respectively. Second, it can also be used to predict the type of crop that better be planted in the current year based on the collected primary (sensors) and secondary (historical) data. Third, users/farmers can remotely initiate irrigation or watering of the crops through the ThingSpeak cloud platform using mobile devices. Moreover, the sensors' real-time data can be downloaded and used for further analysis and insights.

5.3 Future works

In the future, this effort can be improved by using valves to apply nutrients remotely based on the pH sensors result. Moreover, it is also possible to use a camera system to improve monitoring of the whole agricultural field. This work has attempted to make both generic and specific (for garlic) agricultural field monitoring and control mechanisms. Similarly, it can be extended to other crops that can be planted at different geographical areas in the country. Furthermore, crop production or yield monitoring and analysis of the suggested crop type by the classification model would give us better insights about the traditionally used technique named "crop rotation". It is needless to say that using temporally longer agricultural field data using more performance evaluation parameters could give us better insights in the area.

Acknowledgements

We would like to acknowledge the employees of Debre Zeit Agricultural Research Center for their willingness to share the 10-year weather data, among other things.

Competing interests

The authors have declared that they have no competing interest.

Author details

Samuel Zeyede Tefera[1,2] and Asrat Mulatu Beyene[1,3]*

1 Artificial Intelligence and Robotics CoE, Addis Ababa Science and Technology University, Addis Ababa, Ethiopia

2 Department of Software Engineering, Addis Ababa Science and Technology University, Addis Ababa, Ethiopia

3 Department of Electrical and Computer Engineering, Addis Ababa Science and Technology University, Addis Ababa, Ethiopia

*Address all correspondence to: asrat.mulatu@aastu.edu.et

References

[1] Awulachew SB, Ayana M. Performance of irrigation: An assessment at different scales in Ethiopia. Experimental Agriculture. 2011;**47**(S1):57-69

[2] Farooq MS, Riaz S, Abid A, Abid K, Naeem MA. A survey on the role of IoT in agriculture for the implementation of smart farming. IEEE Access. Chennai, India: IEEE; 2019;7:156237-156271

[3] Gebre-Selassie A, Bekele T. A review of Ethiopian agriculture: Roles, policy and small-scale farming systems. Global Growing Casebook: Insights into African Agriculture. 2012;**11**(3):36-65

[4] Welteji D. A critical review of rural development policy of Ethiopia: Access, utilization and coverage. Agriculture & Food Security. 2018;**7**(1):1-6

[5] Kassa M, Andualem TG. Review of Irrigation Practice in Ethiopia. Ethiopia: Lessons from Israel; 2020

[6] Belay M, Bewket W. Traditional irrigation and water management practices in highland Ethiopia: Case study in Dangila woreda. Irrigation and Drainage. 2013;**62**(4):435-448

[7] Campoverde LMS, Tropea M, De Rango F. An IoT based smart irrigation management system using reinforcement learning modeled through a Markov decision process. In: 2021 IEEE/ACM 25th International Symposium on Distributed Simulation and Real Time Applications (DS-RT). Valencia, Spain: IEEE; 2021. pp. 1-4

[8] Madushanki AR, Halgamuge MN, Wirasagoda WS, Ali S. Adoption of the internet of things (IoT) in agriculture and smart farming towards urban greening: A review. International Journal of Advanced Computer Science and Applications. 2019;**10**(4):11-28

[9] Najeeb AG, Kamalakkannan S. Developing an IoT-based data analytics system for predicting soil nutrient degradation level. In: Expert Clouds and Applications. Singapore: Springer; 2022. pp. 125-137

[10] Chowdary TA, Chakravarthy DV, Rupesh RS, Ashish TSC, Charan VHS. Effective implementation of low-cost smart irrigation system. International Journal of Innovative Technology and Exploring Engineering. 2019;**8**(6):1805-1810

[11] Arvind G, Athira VG, Haripriya H, Rani RA, Aravind S. Automated irrigation with advanced seed germination and pest control. In: 2017 IEEE Technological Innovations in ICT for Agriculture and Rural Development (TIAR). Chennai, India: IEEE; 2017. pp. 64-67

[12] Bolfe ÉL, Jorge LADC, Sanches IDA, Luchiari Júnior A, da Costa CC, Victoria DDC, et al. Precision and digital agriculture: Adoption of technologies and perception of Brazilian farmers. Agriculture. 2020;**10**(12):653

[13] Abioye EA, Hensel O, Esau TJ, Elijah O, Abidin MSZ, Ayobami AS, et al. Precision irrigation management using machine learning and digital farming solutions. Agri Engineering. 2022;**4**(1):70-103

[14] Fraga-Lamas P, Celaya-Echarri M, Azpilicueta L, Lopez-Iturri P, Falcone F, Fernández-Caramés TM. Design and empirical validation of a LoRaWAN IoT

smart irrigation system. Proceedings. 2019;**42**(1):62

[15] Risheh A, Jalili A, Nazerfard E. Smart irrigation IoT solution using transfer learning for neural networks. In: 2020 10th International Conference on Computer and Knowledge Engineering (ICCKE). Mashhad, Iran: IEEE; 2020. pp. 342-349

[16] Abdennabi M, Ishaq A, Khalid Haris M, Rachid EA, Surendar S, Muyeen SM. Smart irrigation system using internet of things and cloud computing. Journal of the Saudi Society of Agricultural Sciences. 2024. DOI: 10.1016/j.jssas.2024.02.001

[17] Dubois O. The State of the World's Land and Water Resources for Food and Agriculture: Managing Systems at Risk. Earthscan. Rome, Italy: FAO; 2011

[18] Zerssa G, Feyssa D, Kim DG, Eichler-Löbermann B. Challenges of smallholder farming in Ethiopia and opportunities by adopting climate-smart agriculture. Agriculture. 2021;**11**(3):192

[19] Kumari K, Yadav S. Linear regression analysis study. Journal of the Practice of Cardiovascular Sciences. 2018;**4**(1):33

[20] Yimam AY, Assefa TT, Sishu FK, Tilahun SA, Reyes MR, Prasad PV. Estimating surface and groundwater irrigation potential under different conservation agricultural practices and irrigation systems in the Ethiopian highlands. Water. 2021;**13**(12):1645

[21] Jahanavi G, Sushma UR. Soil classification using machine learning methods and crop [thesis]. Bangalore: CMR Institute of Technology; 2020

[22] Rashid M, Bari BS, Yusup Y, Kamaruddin MA, Khan N. A comprehensive review of crop yield prediction using machine learning approaches with special emphasis on palm oil yield prediction. IEEE Access. 2021;**9**:63406-63439

[23] Rayhana R, Xiao G, Liu Z. Internet of things empowered smart greenhouse farming. IEEE Journal of Radio Frequency Identification. 2020;**4**(3):195-211

[24] Klompenburg VT, Kassahun A, Catal C. Crop yield prediction using machine learning: A systematic literature review. Computers and Electronics in Agriculture. 2020;**177**:105709

[25] Neina D. The role of soil pH in plant nutrition and soil remediation. Applied and Environmental Soil Science. 2019;**2019**:5794869

[26] Lee VE, Liu L, Jin R. Decision trees: Theory and algorithms. In: Data Classification. England, London: Chapman and Hall/CRC; 2014. pp. 115-148

[27] Vanderheiden S. Common but differentiated responsibilities. In: Essential Concepts of Global Environmental Governance. Routledge: IEEE; 2020. pp. 41-43. DOI: 10.1109/JRFID.2020.2984391

[28] Maulud D, Abdulazeez AM. A review on linear regression comprehensive in machine learning. Journal of Applied Science and Technology Trends. 2020;**1**(4):140-147

[29] Rajkumar MN, Abinaya S, Kumar VV. Intelligent irrigation system—An IoT based approach. In: 2017 International Conference on Innovations in Green Energy and Healthcare Technologies (IGEHT). Coimbatore, India: IEEE; 2017. pp. 1-5

[30] Patil P, Sachapara V. Providing smart agricultural solutions/techniques

by using IoT based toolkit. In: 2017 International Conference on Trends in Electronics and Informatics (ICEI). Tirunelveli, India: IEEE; 2017. pp. 327-331

[31] Avinash CM, Girish M, Abhishek V, Manjunath S, Shashi Kumar R. Mobile integrated smart irrigation system using IoT. Journal of Contemporary Issues in Business and Government. 2021;**27**(3):1725-1730

[32] Pooja S, Uday DV, Nagesh UB, Talekar SG. Application of MQTT protocol for real time weather monitoring and precision farming. In: 2017 International Conference on Electrical, Electronics, Communication, Computer, and Optimization Techniques (ICEECCOT). Mysuru, India: IEEE; 2017. pp. 1-6

[33] Rao RN, Sridhar B. IoT based smart crop-field monitoring and automation irrigation system. In: 2018 2nd International Conference on Inventive Systems and Control (ICISC). Coimbatore, India: IEEE; 2018. pp. 478-483

[34] Pernapati K. IoT based low cost smart irrigation system. In: 2018 Second International Conference on Inventive Communication and Computational Technologies (ICICCT). Coimbatore, India: IEEE; 2018. pp. 1312-1315

Chapter 2

Enhancing Smart Parking Management through Machine Learning and AI Integration in IoT Environments

Vesna Knights, Olivera Petrovska and Marija Prchkovska

Abstract

The integration of Internet of Things (IoT) technology has profoundly transformed urban life, particularly in the realm of parking management. Smart parking systems harness the capabilities of IoT to optimize parking space utilization, alleviate congestion, and elevate user experience. This chapter delves into the intricate process of data collection within IoT-enabled smart parking environments, with a specific emphasis on the seamless integration of machine learning and artificial intelligence (AI) techniques. By conducting a comprehensive analysis of various data sources, machine learning algorithms, and AI technologies, this chapter elucidates how smart parking systems leverage intelligent data collection and analysis to enhance operational efficiency and effectiveness. Through the convergence of IoT, machine learning, and AI, smart parking systems are poised to revolutionize urban mobility and drive sustainable urban development.

Keywords: smart parking systems, machine learning, artificial intelligence, IoT environments, data analysis

1. Introduction

The Internet of Things (IoT) has become a groundbreaking technology with extensive applications, profoundly influencing urban infrastructure and services. First introduced by Kevin Ashton in 1999, IoT refers to a network of physical objects embedded with sensors, software, and other technologies, enabling them to connect and exchange data with other devices and systems via the internet [1]. According to Gartner, IoT is one of the top 10 most important strategic technologies globally [2], with Cisco predicting about 50 billion devices connected to the internet or around 3.6 network devices per person by 2023 [3]. Making a comprehensive review [Khanna] and exploring various aspects of applications of IoT [4].

In the realm of urban management, smart parking systems exemplify the practical application of IoT. These systems are designed to address critical issues such as traffic congestion and inefficient use of parking spaces. By leveraging IoT, smart parking systems can monitor and manage parking availability in real-time, enhancing the user experience and contributing to environmental sustainability by reducing the time and fuel wasted searching for parking spots [5, 6]. The integration of IoT with machine learning (ML) and artificial intelligence (AI) further amplifies the capabilities of smart parking systems, enabling them to adapt to changing conditions and user behaviors, offer personalized services, and improve overall operational efficiency [7, 8].

The convergence of IoT, ML, and AI in smart parking systems represents a significant advancement in urban mobility and sustainable development. By collecting and analyzing data from the different sources, it can predict parking occupancy, optimize parking space usage, and implement dynamic pricing strategies [9]. This level of intelligence and adaptability is made possible through sophisticated algorithms and data processing techniques, which are essential for the effective functioning of smart parking solutions.

The need for efficient parking management solutions is underscored by the growing urban population and the corresponding increase in vehicle ownership. Conventional parking systems are often inadequate in meeting the demands of modern urban environments, leading to issues such as congestion, pollution, and frustration among drivers. Smart parking systems, have ability to provide real-time information and optimize parking resources and to offer a viable solution to these challenges [10, 11].

Previous research has demonstrated the effectiveness of smart parking systems in various contexts. For instance, the application of big data technologies in traffic monitoring and management has shown significant improvements in handling large volumes of traffic data [12]. It underscores the importance of integrating GIS and big data technologies for effective traffic data analysis and visualization [13, 14]. Furthermore, demonstrates how IoT, cloud technology, and deep learning models can predict parking space availability, reducing the traffic congestion and fuel consumption [15]. The recent studies on smart parking implementations in different cities worldwide provide a broader perspective on the advancements and effectiveness of smart parking systems in urban environments.

Barcelona has integrated various smart city initiatives, including smart parking systems that utilize IoT-enabled sensors and mobile applications [16]. These systems provide real-time parking availability, reducing traffic congestion and enhancing urban mobility. The city's Urban Mobility Plan aims to have over 80% of journeys made via sustainable modes by 2024 [17, 18].

The SFpark project uses dynamic pricing based on real-time demand data. This approach optimizes parking space usage, reduces cruising for parking, and lowers greenhouse gas emissions. The integration of autonomous parking solutions with IoT technologies has further enhanced the efficiency and effectiveness of the city's parking management [19–21].

Amsterdam's smart parking systems employ a combination of sensors and cameras to monitor parking space usage. Real-time data is provided to users via mobile apps, allowing for automated payment and reservation of parking spaces. These systems have significantly improved the city's ability to manage high traffic densities and optimize parking resources [13, 22, 23].

Singapore has developed a unified platform that integrates various parking systems across the city. This platform collects data from multiple sources, including IoT sensors and cameras, to provide real-time parking information. The system supports electronic payments and dynamic pricing to manage parking demand effectively [13, 24–26].

London utilizes Automatic Number Plate Recognition (ANPR) technology to monitor and manage parking spaces. This technology provides real-time data on parking availability and aids in enforcing parking regulations. The city's smart parking system also integrates mobile payment options, streamlining the parking process for users and improving overall efficiency [27].

This innovative approach combines IoT and deep learning to provide accurate and reliable predictions for parking availability, showcasing the potential of advanced technologies in improving urban mobility solutions.

Defiantly intelligent vehicles and mobile robot guidance and control systems have provided valuable insights into the application of ML and AI in transportation [28–30]. The trajectory following and obstacle avoidance have highlighted the importance of precise data collection and analysis in optimizing processes and enhancing the performance of intelligent systems [31–33]. This technological paradigm shift the foundation for the development and implementation of smart systems across various domains, such as smart home [34] agriculture, healthcare, industries, and smart cities [35]. Challenges of increasing the security of IoT will be always a topic [4, 36].

This chapter explores the integration of IoT, ML, and AI in smart parking systems, aiming to address critical urban issues like traffic congestion and inefficient parking space utilization. The study hypothesizes that the convergence of these technologies will significantly enhance parking management by providing real-time data analysis and predictions.

In Skopje, Republic of North Macedonia, the implementation of smart parking systems is particularly relevant due to the city's evolving urban landscape and increasing vehicular traffic. By adopting advanced technologies such as electromagnetic sensors, ANPR cameras, and mobile applications, can enhance its parking infrastructure and improve the overall quality of urban life [37–39]. The real case serves as a practical example of how IoT, ML, and AI can be integrated to create efficient, user-friendly, and sustainable urban solutions.

2. Design of smart parking systems

An intelligent parking system has been developed to address the challenges associated with both street parking and parking garages. Understanding the various elements that contribute to the development of such a system is crucial for comprehending how smart parking operates.

Sensors: Installed on roads and grounds, these devices help parking lot managers track customer habits and determine the suitability of available spots for different needs. They detect vehicles and update the status of parking spaces.

Cameras: Positioned in strategic locations within the parking lot, cameras gage the size and motion of vehicles. They capture images and detect motion, providing visual data to the central server.

Parking meters: These act as intermediaries between owners and customers, providing authorization and payment details to operators. They authorize parking and process payments.

Centralized server: The server receives data from sensors and images from cameras. It processes this information and manages data interactions, relaying relevant details to users via mobile apps.

Parking management software: This software communicates with stakeholders, providing real-time information on parking spaces. It updates parking information and notifies users, ensuring efficient management of parking resources.

Smart mobile apps: Mobile apps facilitate transaction handling, enabling users to find parking spaces on the street and in garages.

The relationships and interactions among these components are depicted in **Figure 1**, which provides a class diagram of the Smart Parking System. This diagram is crucial as it illustrates how the different elements work together to create an efficient and intelligent parking management system, highlighting the structural design and the interactions between sensors, cameras, parking meters, the central server, and parking management software.

In the context of urban environments, smart parking systems exemplify the practical application of IoT, aiming to address critical issues such as traffic congestion and inefficient use of parking spaces. These systems utilize a variety of sensors and communication technologies, such as Bluetooth, Radio Frequency Identification (RFID), and Wi-Fi, to monitor and manage parking availability in real-time [40–42]. The integration of IoT in parking management not only enhances the user experience but also contributes to environmental sustainability by reducing the time and fuel wasted searching for parking spots.

To classify smart parking systems and integrate networking and layers, we need to understand the different components and how they interact within the system. Smart parking systems can be classified into different layers: Application Layer, Network Layer, Transaction Layer, and Physical Layer. The sequence diagram in **Figure 2**

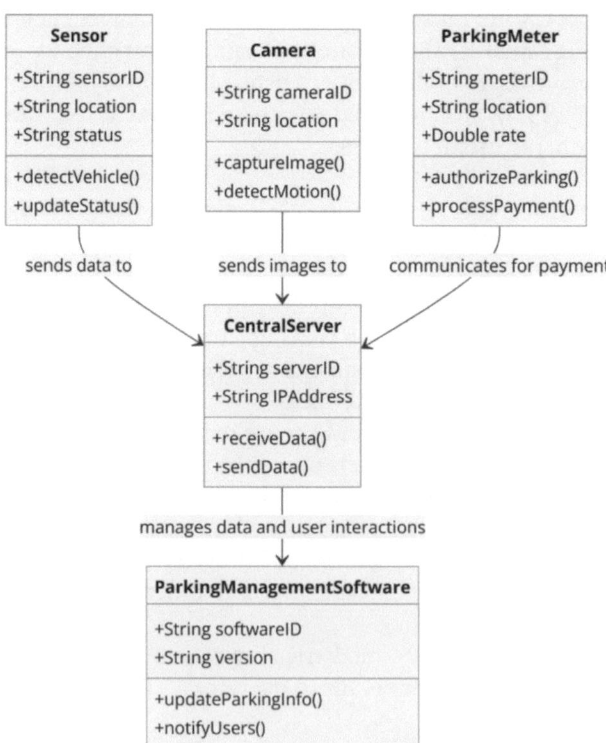

Figure 1.
Class diagram of the smart parking system.

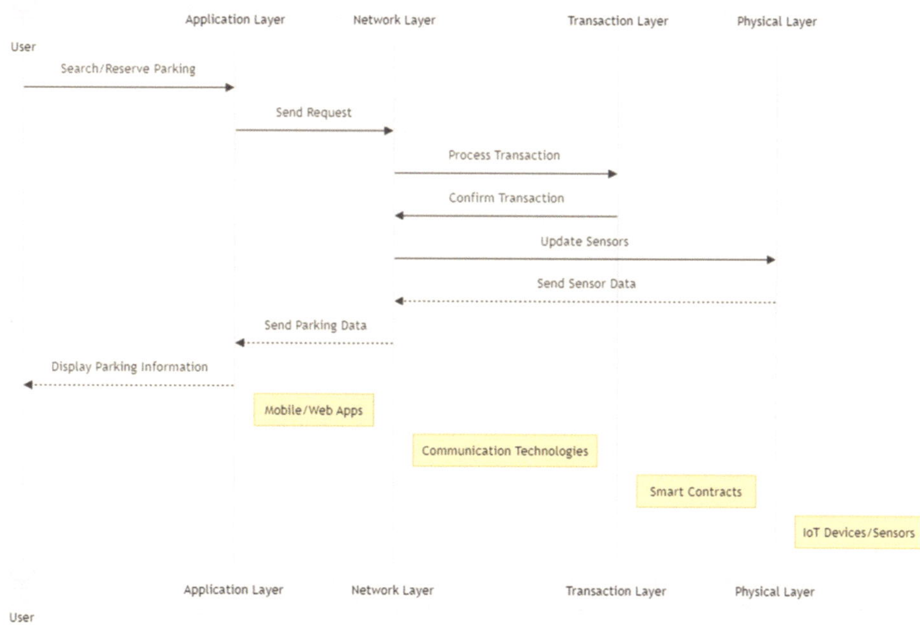

Figure 2.
Sequence diagram of architecture of smart parking systems.

illustrates the architecture of integrated smart parking systems, showing how these layers interact to provide a seamless and efficient parking experience.

Application layer: User interaction with the system; Mobile and web applications for searching and reserving parking spots.

Network layer: Ensures communication between the application, parking centers, and IoT devices. Utilizes technologies like LAN, WAN, Bluetooth, Wi-Fi, 4G, and 5G.

Transaction layer: Handles transactions securely using smart contracts and consensus mechanisms. Updates the distributed ledger.

Physical layer: Consists of sensors and devices that gather and transmit data. Includes parking sensors, cameras, and other IoT devices.

Figure 2 visualizes the data flow and interaction between different layers within the smart parking system. It helps in understanding the comprehensive architecture and how various technologies and components work together to deliver a user-friendly and efficient parking management solution.

3. Data integration in adaptive learning of smart parking systems

Adaptive learning refers to systems that can adjust their operations based on data and feedback, improving over time. In the context of smart parking, adaptive learning can optimize parking space usage, predict future occupancy, and implement dynamic pricing strategies.

Smart parking systems operate by collecting data from multiple sources, to provide accurate information on parking space availability. This data is then processed using advanced machine learning (ML) and artificial intelligence (AI) techniques to predict parking occupancy, optimize parking space usage, and implement dynamic pricing

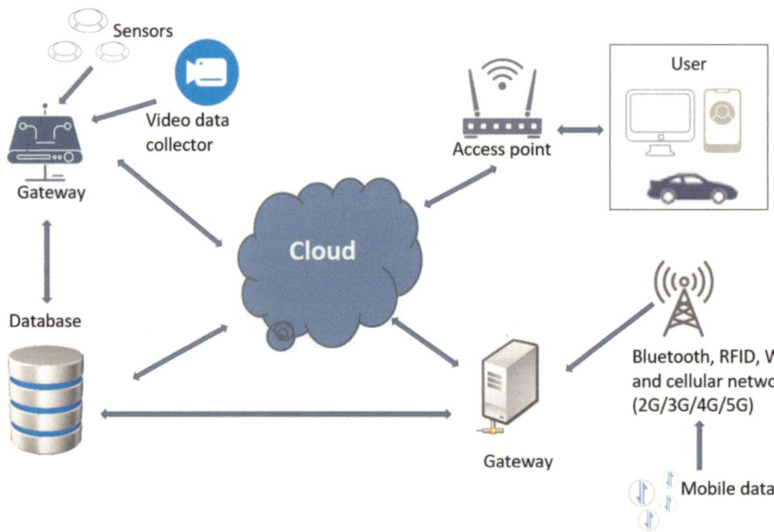

Figure 3.
Smart parking system model.

strategies [43–46]. By leveraging these technologies, smart parking systems can adapt to changing conditions and user behaviors, offering personalized services and improving overall operational efficiency.

The diagram in **Figure 3** illustrates the model of a smart parking system, highlighting the flow of data from sensors and mobile data collectors through gateways and the cloud to the end-users. This model shows how the integration of various components and communication technologies enables real-time monitoring and management of parking spaces.

Figure 3 provides a comprehensive view of the system architecture, depicting the integration of various components and communication technologies in real-time monitoring and management of parking spaces. Here are the elements in the diagram:

- *Sensors*: Collect data on parking space occupancy and transmit this information to the video data collector.
- *Video data collector*: Gathers video data from cameras and sends it to the cloud for processing.
- *Gateway*: Acts as an intermediary, transmitting data between sensors, the database, and the cloud.
- *Database*: Stores collected data for analysis and retrieval.
- *Cloud*: Central hub for data processing and storage, facilitating communication between different system components.
- *Access point*: Provides connectivity between the cloud and user devices, allowing users to access parking information.
- *User*: Accesses parking information via mobile and web applications, making informed decisions about parking space usage.

- *Communication technologies*: Utilize Bluetooth, RFID, Wi-Fi, and cellular networks (2G/3G/4G/5G) to transmit data between devices.
- *Mobile data*: Enables real-time data transmission from user devices to the cloud.

By integrating ML and AI into IoT-enabled smart parking systems, we can significantly enhance urban mobility, reduce congestion, and promote sustainable development. The advanced data collection and analysis techniques allow for accurate, real-time information on parking space availability, optimizing resource utilization and implementing dynamic pricing strategies. ML algorithms analyze parking data to determine parking status and predict future occupancy, enabling smarter traffic management.

Machine learning methods in smart parking systems can be based on different types of data collected from various sources, such as images, GPS signals, environmental sensors, and time-based data. Each data type provides unique insights into parking dynamics:

SPS based on Computer vision/image processing: Utilizing camera networks, these systems extract information such as parking occupancy status, license plate recognition, and facial recognition for payment and security. They are particularly suitable for open parking lots, although they can be affected by occlusion, shadows, and lighting changes [47].

SPS based on Global positioning system (GPS): GPS guides users to available parking spots and can predict parking occupancy and traffic congestion. While suitable for open parking lots, GPS accuracy can vary, and it is less effective in indoor spaces [12]. Advantages of GPS are, highly effective for open parking lots and provides real-time location data. Challenges can be, GPS accuracy, especially in indoor or densely built environments, making it less effective for covered parking areas. This kind of example is navigation systems guiding drivers to available parking spots. Real-time traffic and parking congestion prediction [48].

SPS based on Wireless sensor networks (WSN): consists of wirelessly connected sensor nodes that monitor various environmental data facilities. These sensors are highly flexible, adaptable, and cost-effective, making them popular among SPS developers [49]. This involves connecting sensors to processing units, either through wired or wireless technologies such as ZigBee, Wi-Fi, and mobile networks (3G/4G) [50–52].

Historical and real-time reservation data: Connects end-users to SPS for tasks like data visualization, parking reservation, and payment, primarily relying on wireless connectivity like 3G/4G/5G, Wi-Fi, and Device-to-Device (D2D) communication. This method includes information such as the entry and exit times of vehicles, the total duration of vehicle occupancy, and the availability of parking spaces. Both historical and real-time data are used to improve parking management. Enables predictive analytics for better parking management and dynamic pricing strategies.

By integrating IoT with machine learning and AI, smart parking systems can significantly enhance urban mobility, reduce congestion, and promote sustainable development.

4. Methodology: Real-case

Skopje capital city of North Macedonia, has open and closed parking areas managed by ramps for access control. The public enterprise City Parking Skopje implemented 9396 parking spaces to cater to the needs of residents in regulating inactive traffic and improving parking conditions. The city's parking areas are organized into four zones based on restriction levels and proximity to the city center: first degree (red zone), second degree (yellow zone), third degree (green zone), and fourth degree (white zone).

To analyze the parking situation in Skopje, data were collected from three parking locations within the city center: red zone, yellow zone, and green zone.

4.1 Data collection

The data collection involved a manual counting method called the "Entry-Exit" method. This method entails recording the number of vehicles entering and exiting the parking area over a specified time period. The data collection was conducted over seven consecutive days, from 2019 to 2022 year. This timeframe covers both peak and off-peak hours, providing a detailed understanding of daily parking patterns.

4.1.1 Parameters measured

Initial occupancy (i): The count of vehicles present in the parking area at the beginning of the observation period; Vehicle entry: The count of vehicles entering the parking area during the observation period; Vehicle exit: The count of vehicles exiting the parking area during the observation period.

4.2 Data preprocessing and analysis

The data collected were processed to calculate the occupancy and utilization rates of the parking facilities. The formula used to calculate the occupancy at any given time is:

$$Z = i + \text{Entry} - \text{Exit} \tag{1}$$

where Z is the occupancy, i is the initial number of parked vehicles, and Entry and Exit are the counts of vehicles entering and exiting the parking area, respectively.

The process of methodology and the steps of machine learning to enable smart parking is shown in **Figure 4**.

The process begins with collecting the parking data set. This data includes various information about parking such as entry and exit times, occupancy, and other relevant variables.

Data preprocessing: The raw data collected is preprocessed to clean and format it appropriately. This step may include handling missing values, normalizing the data, and removing any inconsistencies to ensure the data is suitable for analysis.

Data splitting: The preprocessed data is split into two sets: training data and test data. Typically, 75% of the data is used for training the model, and the remaining 25% is used for testing its performance.

Building models are made base on supervised machine learn algorithms and regression method. Given that dataset is data that is time series as the most suitable models are taken Ridge Regression, RandomForestRegressor with lagged features for time series data and, Multi-Layer Perceptron (MLP) Regressor with neural network architecture algorithms to develop predictive models.

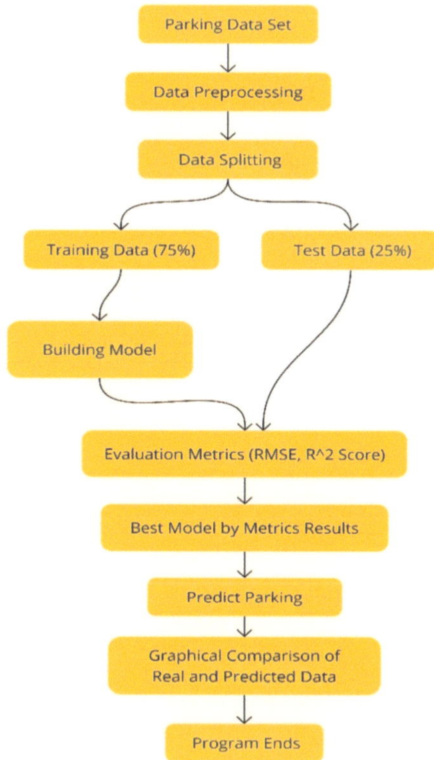

Figure 4.
Algorithm of the machine learning process for data analysis of parking place.

The Ridge Regression is a linear regression which includes a regularization term in order to prevent overfitting. The regularization term, also known as the L2 penalty, adds a constraint on the coefficients of the model. The objective of ridge regression is to reduce the sum of squared residuals while also constraining the magnitude of the coefficients.

Let us denote the following:

$$\hat{y} = X\beta + b \tag{2}$$

$\hat{y}$ is predicted target variable, X is matrix of input features, β is a vector of coeficients, and b is intercept term.

In Ridge Regression, the coefficients β are determined by minimizing the combined error between the observed and predicted target values, while also penalizing large coefficients to prevent overfitting. This is achieved by solving the optimization problem expressed in the equation:

$$\min \beta \left(\sum_{i=1}^{N} (y_i - \hat{y})^2 + \alpha \sum_{i=1}^{p} \beta_j^2 \right) \tag{3}$$

A Random Forest Regressor is an ensemble learning method that operates by constructing multiple decision trees during training and outputting the average prediction of the individual trees. It is highly effective for regression tasks and can be adapted for time series forecasting by incorporating lagged features. It uses past values of the time series (lagged features) to predict future values. By averaging the predictions of multiple decision trees, it provides a robust and accurate forecast. This method is effective for capturing complex patterns in time series data without requiring assumptions about the underlying data distribution.

Given a time series data {yt} at time t, to forecast future values of the time series, it is used past values (lagged features) as inputs. For example, to predict y_t, the features are:

$$y_t, y_{t-1}, y_{t-2}, \dots y_{t-p} \tag{4}$$

where p is the number of lags.

For each time step t, we construct a feature vector.

$\{X_t\}$ consisting of lagged values of the time series:

$$X_t = \begin{pmatrix} y_{t-1} \\ y_{t-2} \\ \cdot \\ \cdot \\ \cdot \\ y_{t-p} \end{pmatrix} \tag{5}$$

For each time step t from p to T (where T is the total number of time steps), create a feature vector X_t and the corresponding target value Y_t.

For training set:

Input features:

$$x_{p+1}, x_{p+2}, \dots x_T \tag{6}$$

Constructing the Training Set for each t from p to T for input features:

$$X_{p+1} = \begin{pmatrix} y_p \\ y_{p=1} \\ \cdot \\ \cdot \\ \cdot \\ y_1 \end{pmatrix} X_{p+2} = \begin{pmatrix} y_{p+1} \\ y_p \\ \cdot \\ \cdot \\ \cdot \\ y_2 \end{pmatrix} X_T = \begin{pmatrix} y_{T-1} \\ y_{T-2} \\ \cdot \\ \cdot \\ \cdot \\ y_{T-p} \end{pmatrix} \tag{7}$$

Target values:

$$y_{p+1}, y_{p+2}, \dots y_T \tag{8}$$

The model f predicts the future value $\hat{y}_t$ based on the input feature vector x_t:

$$\hat{y}_t = f(X_t) \tag{9}$$

Individual decision trees: Each decision tree $h_i(x_i)$ in the forest is trained on a bootstrapped sample of the training data.

Random subset of features: At each split in the tree, a random subset of features is selected, and the best split is chosen from this subset.

Aggregating predictions: The prediction of the Random Forest Regressor is the average of the predictions of the individual trees:

$$\hat{y} = \frac{1}{n}\sum_{i=1}^{n} h_i(x_i) \tag{10}$$

where n is the number of trees.

A Multi-Layer Perceptron (MLP), consists of the input and output layer, and between them one or more hidden layers. Each layer is composed of nodes (neurons). The neurons in one layer are connected to those in the subsequent layer through weights.

Input Layer to Hidden Layer.

Input features: $X = [x_1, x_2, \ldots x_n]^{T.}$

Weights $W^{[1]}$

Biases $b^{[1]}$

Transformation to the hidden layer:

$$Z^{[1]} = W^{[1]}X + b^{[1]} \tag{11}$$

In matrix form:

$$Z^{[1]} = \begin{bmatrix} W_{11}^{[1]} & W_{12}^{[1]} & \cdots & W_{1n}^{[1]} \\ W_{21}^{[1]} & W_{22}^{[1]} & \cdots & W_{2n}^{[1]} \\ \vdots & \vdots & \ddots & \vdots \\ W_{h1}^{[1]} & W_{h2}^{[1]} & \cdots & W_{hn}^{[1]} \end{bmatrix} \begin{bmatrix} x_1 \\ x_2 \\ \vdots \\ x_n \end{bmatrix} + \begin{bmatrix} b_1^{[1]} \\ b_2^{[1]} \\ \vdots \\ b_h^{[1]} \end{bmatrix} \tag{12}$$

Activation Function: $A^{[1]} = f\left(Z^{[1]}\right)$

Hidden Layer to Output Layer

Weights $W^{[2]}$

Biases $b^{[2]}$

Transformation to the hidden layer:

$$Z^{[2]} = W^{[2]}A^1 + b^{[2]} \tag{13}$$

In matrix form:

$$Z^{[2]} = \left[W_{11}^{[2]}\, W_{12}^{[2]} \ldots W_{1h}^{[2]}\right] \begin{bmatrix} A_1^{[1]} \\ A_2^{[1]} \\ \vdots \\ A_h^1 \end{bmatrix} + \left[b^{[2]}\right] \tag{14}$$

Output:

$$\hat{y}_t = Z^{[2]} \tag{15}$$

Evaluation metrics (RMSE, R^2 Score): The trained models are evaluated using metrics such as RMSE (Root Mean Square Error) and R^2 Score (Coefficient of Determination). These metrics help in understanding how well the model is performing in terms of accuracy and variance explanation.

The RMSE presents a measure of the differences between the values predicted by the model and the actual values. It is determined by taking the square root of the mean of the squared discrepancies between the predicted values and the actual values. The formula for RMSE is:

$$RMSE = \sqrt{\frac{1}{n}\sum_{i=1}^{n}(y_i - \hat{y})^2} \tag{16}$$

Where
n is the number of data points
y_i is the actual value
$\hat{y}_i$ is the predicted value
R^2 Score: is a statistical measure that indicates the proportion of the variance in the dependent variable that is predictable from the independent variables. Value of R^2 Score is between 0 and 1, where 1 indicates that the regression predictions perfectly fit the data. The formula for R^2 Score is

$$R^2 = 1 - \frac{\sum (y_i - \hat{y})^2}{\sum (y_i - \bar{y})^2} \tag{17}$$

$\overline{y_i}$ is the actual value
R^2 Score: Reflects how well the model explains the variance in the data. Higher R^2 values indicate better explanatory power.

These metrics aid in evaluating the accuracy and reliability of parking space availability predictions, guiding the selection of the most suitable machine learning model.

Best model by metrics results: Based on the evaluation metrics, the best-performing model is selected. This model is considered the most suitable for predicting parking availability and occupancy.

Predict parking: The selected model is then used to predict parking availability based on new data or unseen data. This step involves using the model to make predictions on parking occupancy.

Graphical comparison of real and predicted data: A graphical comparison is made between the real (actual) data and the predicted data to visually assess the performance of the model. This helps in understanding how close the predictions are to the actual values.

5. Results

The data collected provided insights into the hourly variation in parking occupancy at each location. To visualize the distribution of vehicle data across different junctions in the parking place, we utilized Python's seaborn and matplotlib libraries to create histograms with Kernel Density Estimate (KDE) overlays. The histograms help in understanding the frequency and probability distribution of vehicle counts at various parking places, providing insights into traffic patterns and parking demand. On the x-axis, the number of vehicles is represented, while on the y-axis, the probability is shown. **Figure 5** presents the visualization of vehicle distribution for different parking places: parking place 1, which is the red zone, parking place 2, which is the yellow zone, and parking place 3, which is the green zone.

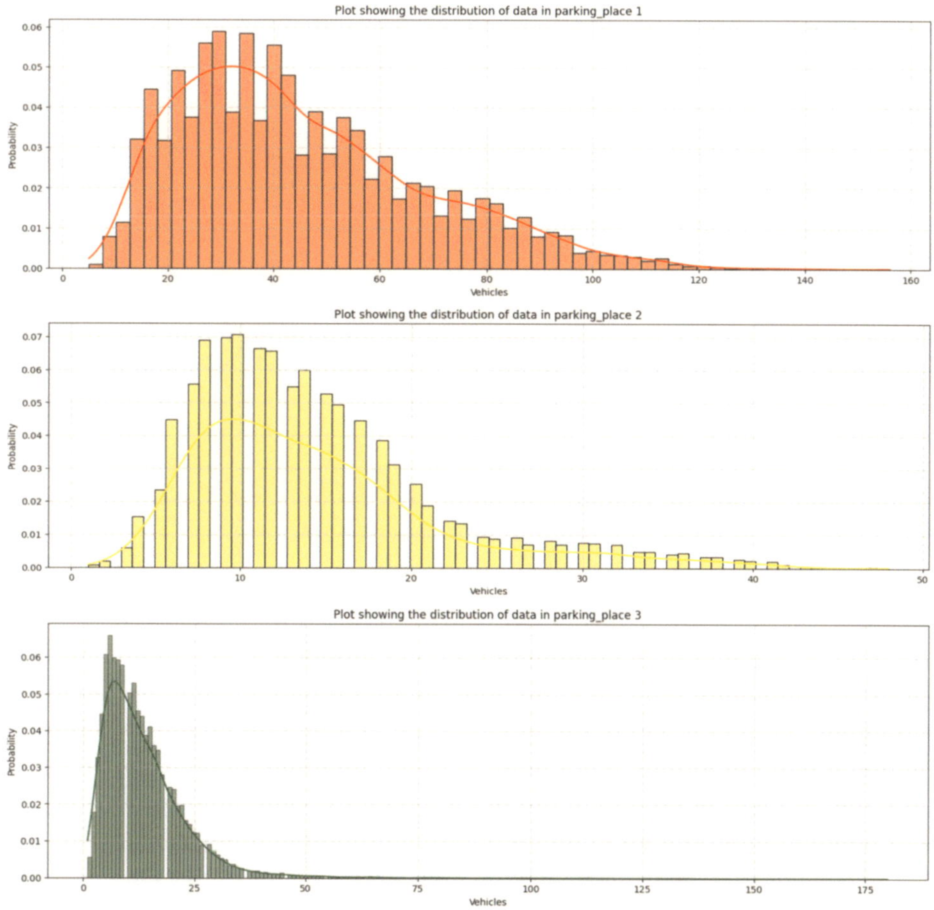

Figure 5.
Vehicle distribution for different parking places, parking place 1 (red zone), parking place 2 (yellow zone), and parking place 3 (green zone).

These visualizations are crucial for identifying trends and patterns in vehicle distribution, which can inform decisions related to traffic management and smart parking solutions. To analyze and visualize the monthly sum of vehicle data for different parking places, we used Python's matplotlib library to create a series of line plots. These plots provide a clear depiction of vehicle counts over time, allowing us to observe trends and variations across different parking places.

Each subplot provides a visual representation of the monthly summed vehicle counts, allowing for comparison and analysis of vehicle trends across the different parking places. The use of different colors for each parking place enhances the clarity and distinction between the plots.

These visualizations are crucial for identifying patterns in vehicle distribution, which can inform decisions related to traffic management and smart parking solutions.

Figure 6 displays the monthly dynamics of the number of vehicles in three different parking places (parking place 1, parking place 2, and parking place 3) from January 2020 to July 2021. Each subplot represents the vehicle counts for a specific parking place over time, using different colors for clear distinction.

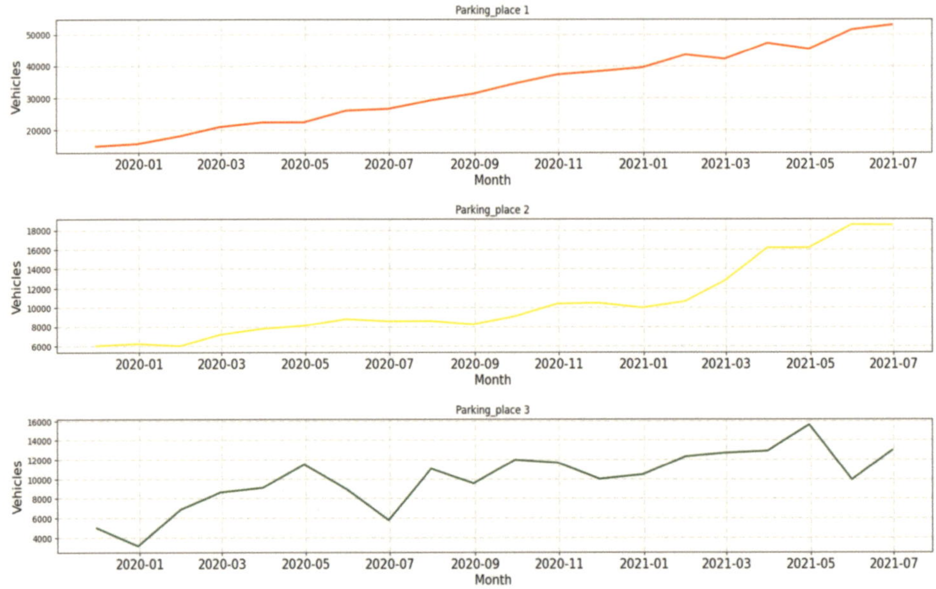

Figure 6.
Dinamics of amounts of vehicles by parking places (each parking place by month).

Parking place 1 (red line): This diagram shows a steady increase in the number of vehicles over the observed period. The vehicle count starts at approximately 20,000 in January 2020 and gradually rises to about 50,000 by July 2021. The consistent upward trend suggests a growing demand for parking at this location, possibly due to increased traffic or a rise in the number of events and activities in the area.

Parking place 2 (yellow line): In contrast to parking place 1, this plot shows a more stable vehicle count with minor fluctuations until late 2020. From early 2021, there's a noticeable increase in the number of vehicles, rising from around 6000 to approximately 18,000 by July 2021. The initial stability followed by a significant increase indicates that parking place 2 experienced a sudden surge in demand, which could be due to changes in nearby attractions, improved accessibility, or other local developments.

Parking place 3 (green line): demonstrates more variability compared to the other two parking places. The data shows fluctuations throughout the period, with peaks around mid-2020 and early 2021, and a notable rise toward July 2021. The fluctuating pattern suggests that parking place 3 may be influenced by seasonal events, temporary closures, or other periodic factors affecting its use. The increase toward the end of the observed period might indicate a shift in traffic patterns or enhanced usage.

The performance of each model was evaluated using two primary metrics: the coefficient R^2 Score and RMSE. These metrics provide insights into the models' predictive accuracy and precision. **Table 1** summarizes the performance metrics of the machine learning models used in the study, such as Ridge Regression, RandomForestRegressor, and Multi-Layer Perceptron, across different parking zones.

The R^2 score is thee coefficient of determination, indicates how well the model explains the variance in the data. The closer the R^2 score is to 1, the better the model's performance. A higher R^2 score means the model can explain more of the variability in the target variable.

Model	Parking zone	R^2 Score	RMSE
Ridge regression	red	0.621827	14.181326
	yellow	0.521465	5.095181
	green	0.250087	8.830870
RandomForestRegressor - Lag model	red	0.970134	3.973837
	yellow	0.885717	2.522930
	green	0.725747	5.696169
Neural network (Multi-layer perceptron)			
	red	0.938788	5.847090
	yellow	0.864009	2.773242
	green	0.751293	5.071122

Table 1.
Metrics results of the models across parking zones.

- *Ridge regression*: The R^2 scores range from 0.250087 to 0.621827, indicating that this model explains a moderate amount of variance in the data, with better performance in the red zone and lower performance in the green zone.
- *RandomForestRegressor - Lag model*: This model shows high R^2 scores, ranging from 0.725747 to 0.970134, indicating excellent performance across all zones, particularly in the red zone.
- *Neural network (Multi-layer perceptron)*: The R^2 scores are also high, ranging from 0.751293 to 0.938788, showing good performance across all zones, especially in the red zone.

RMSE measures the average magnitude of the errors between predicted and actual values. A lower RMSE indicates better model performance, as it signifies that the predictions are closer to the actual values.

- *Ridge regression*: The RMSE values range from 5.095181 to 14.181326, indicating that the predictions have a higher average error, particularly in the red zone.
- *RandomForestRegressor - Lag model*: This model shows low RMSE values, ranging from 2.522930 to 5.696169, indicating more accurate predictions, especially in the yellow zone.
- *Neural network (Multi-layer perceptron)*: The RMSE values range from 2.773242 to 5.847090, showing that the model makes relatively accurate predictions, particularly in the yellow zone.

At **Figure 7** is presented the model performs. The performs on the “red” zone is with the highest R^2 score (0.970134) and a moderate RMSE (3.973837).

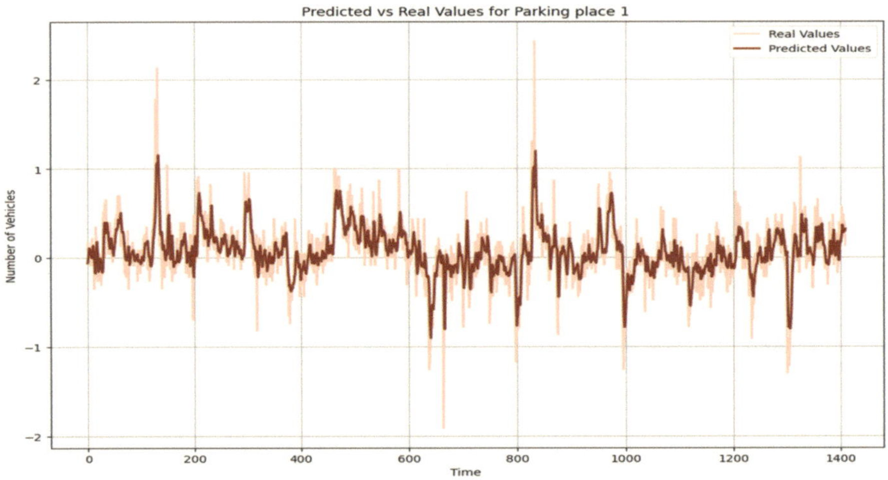

Figure 7.
Predicted vs. real values for parking place 1 (red zone).

The graph shows the predicted values closely following the trend of the real values. The alignment between the predicted and real values indicates that the model effectively captures the patterns and fluctuations in vehicle numbers over time.

Occasional spikes and dips in the real values are also reflected in the predicted values, demonstrating the model's ability to respond to variations. However, some discrepancies exist, particularly in the peaks and troughs, which is expected in any predictive model.

Figure 8 illustrates the performance of the predictive model for parking place 2 (Yellow Zone) by comparing the predicted values (dark yellow line) against the real values (light yellow line) over time. The model performs well on the "yellow" zone, with a good R^2 score (0.885717) and the lowest RMSE (2.522930), indicating the most accurate predictions.

Both figures show that the predicted values closely follow the real values, but **Figure 7** has occasional larger discrepancies in peaks. **Figure 8** demonstrates stronger

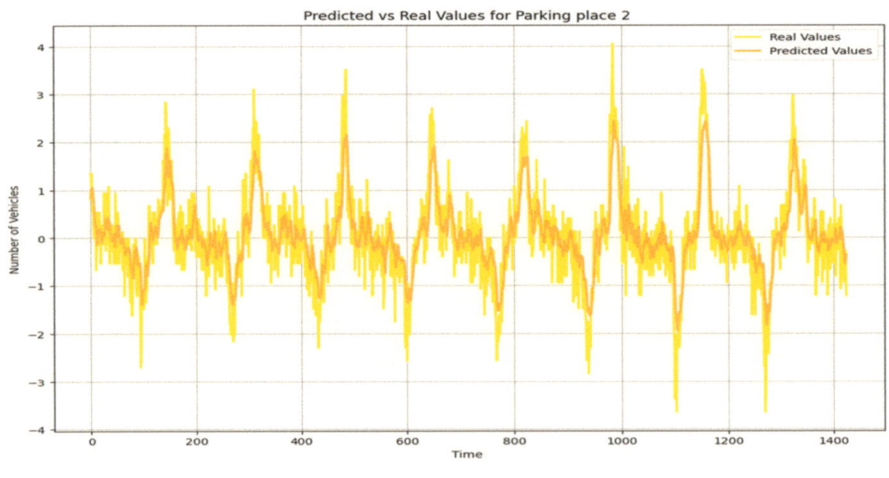

Figure 8.
Predicted vs. real values for parking place 2 (yellow zone).

Figure 9.
Predicted vs. real values for parking place 3 (green zone).

alignment in capturing peaks and troughs. Both models are highly useful for real-time management, but the model for the Red Zone (**Figure 7**) shows slightly better overall variance explanation, while the model for the Yellow Zone (**Figure 8**) has a lower average prediction error, indicating more precise predictions.

Figure 9 illustrates the performance of the predictive model for parking place 3 (Green Zone) by comparing the predicted values (dark green line) against the real values (light green line) over time.

The model performs the worst on the "green" dataset, with the lowest R^2 score (0.725747) and the highest RMSE (5.696169). The graph shows that the predicted values (dark green line) generally follow the trend of the real values (light green line). However, there are noticeable discrepancies, particularly around the peaks and troughs, where the model fails to capture some of the extreme variations in the real values. Despite these discrepancies, the model captures the overall pattern and central tendencies in vehicle numbers over time, indicating less accurate predictions compared to the other datasets.

6. Proposed development of a smart parking solution for Skopje for future work

Based on the data collected and the observed peak parking hours, a smart parking system utilizing mobile applications is proposed. The model follows the example of Barcelona [13, 53], where wireless sensors provide real-time parking status updates through a mobile app. This system includes:

- Electromagnetic sensors at each parking spot to detect occupancy,
- ANPR cameras for vehicle identification,
- Infrared cameras at entry and exit points for monitoring,
- A mobile app for users to check availability, make reservations, and manage payments.

Implementing this smart parking system will reduce traffic congestion during peak hours, streamline the parking search process, and provide real-time parking information to drivers. The intelligent system will modernize vehicle control and reduce the need for human labor, making it an efficient and sustainable solution for Skopje's growing urban infrastructure.

The development of the smart parking system involves installing wireless sensors and providing real-time updates on the status of parking locations through a mobile application. As the most appropriate and acceptable, I suggest that it be applied to the selected locations in Skopje.

The following **Figure 10** shows the architecture of the proposed smart parking model.

The way this proposed smart parking system works is as follows: first, the user requests information from the mobile application. In this case, the user can request where the parking is available, the location of the available parking space, payment information, etc. Sensors placed in each parking space detect whether the parking space is available or unavailable and transmit the information wirelessly to the database and then to the user. The mobile application then displays information stored from the database in the server and resolves the user's query in real time. Vehicles can be parked in the available space and the user can pay for the parking space and locate the car at any time using the mobile application.

The electromagnetic sensors are installed in each parking space, in each of the parking locations, which detect the status of each parking space and send all the information about the occupancy to the central management unit. To deliver the occupancy status of each parking space, sensors are connected to an IoT network. The sensors work on batteries and continuously register the presence of a vehicle in the parking space and wirelessly send the data to the receiver. A receiver operating in the 865–867 Mhz range updates this server occupancy data to the control center over the Internet using a wired network, as shown in **Figure 11**.

The identification of the vehicles arriving or leaving the parking lot is done using an ANPR camera (**Figure 11**). ANPR stands for Automatic Number Plate Recognition

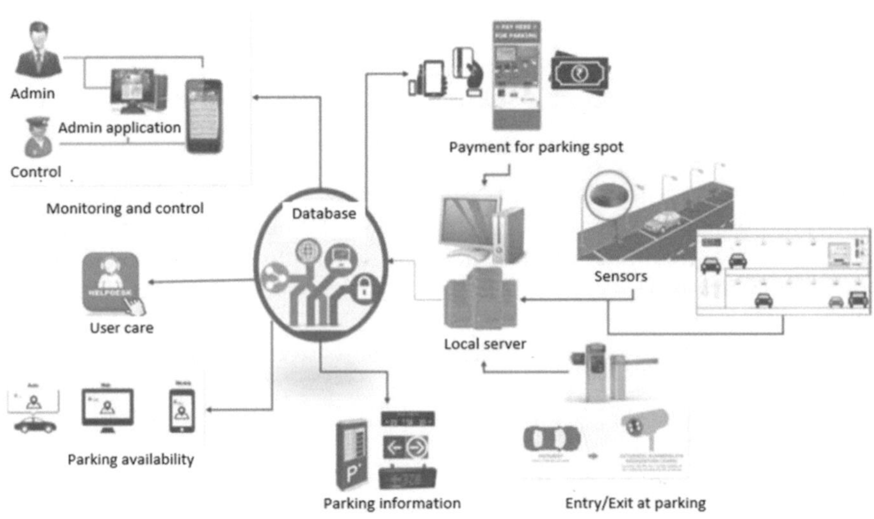

Figure 10.
Proposed development of a smart parking system.

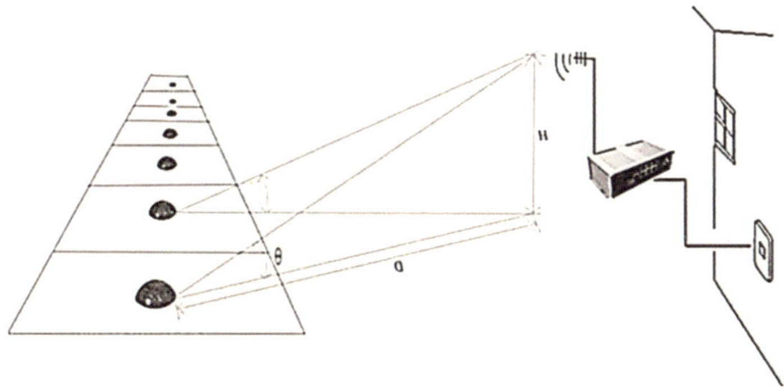

Figure 11.
An example of sensor and receiver placement in a parking location.

and contains the technology to identify a vehicle by number plate. With the implementation of automatic license plate recognition cameras, the technology can scan a license plate and forward the associated action to the management system. This allows for a modernized version of vehicle control and limits the need for human labor given the stand-alone nature of ANPR technology. In addition, the parking lot has cameras (based on infrared technology) with the ability to zoom, located at the entry and exit points to monitor the parking zone. Any unauthorized entry of the vehicle that does not go through plate recognition can be easily verified by the operator.

Users can check the availability of the parking zone, as well as get information about the location and availability of parking locations through the mobile application installed in their mobile phones. The mobile application also shows users the occupancy of parking zones in real time.

As described above, the mobile application offers two ways for drivers to select a desired parking location, by searching for parking locations through the nearby button and by entering the address of the desired parking location, as shown in **Figure 12**.

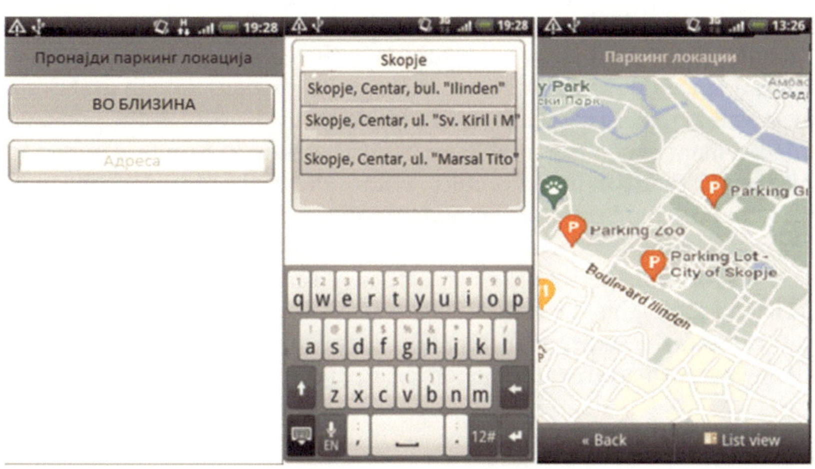

Figure 12.
Smart parking app.

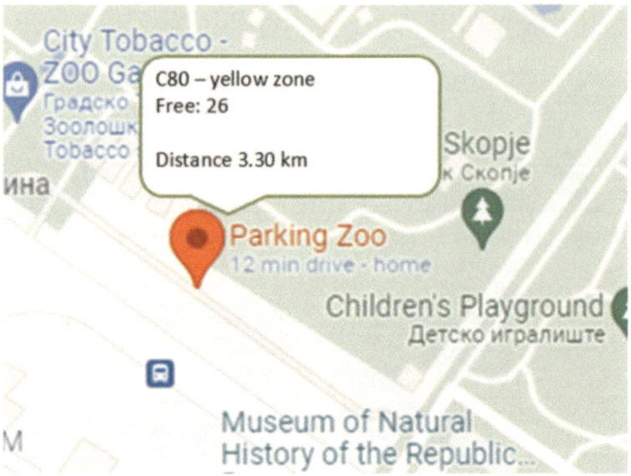

Figure 13.
Information about parking location 2 (Zone C80 – yellow zone).

After they select the desired address, the coordinates are sent to the management system which then updates the data in real time. If the user selects the nearby button, the GPS system locates the user's current location and the application displays the distance and availability of parking locations as shown in **Figures 12** and **13**.

7. Conclusions

The integration of IoT, machine learning, and artificial intelligence within smart parking systems offers a promising solution to the growing challenges of urban mobility and parking management. This chapter has demonstrated how leveraging these advanced technologies can optimize parking space utilization, reduce traffic congestion, and enhance the overall user experience.

The data analysis and machine learning models applied in this study have provided valuable insights into parking occupancy patterns and the effectiveness of predictive algorithms. The RandomForestRegressor with lagged features exhibited superior performance across all parking zones, making it the most effective model for predicting vehicle counts. The Neural Network (Multi-layer Perceptron) also showed good performance and is a viable alternative, while Ridge Regression, though useful, did not perform as well as the other two models, especially for the data of the green zone.

The deployment of such an intelligent parking system in Skopje is poised to modernize the city's urban infrastructure, reduce the environmental impact of traffic congestion, and promote sustainable urban development. By continuously monitoring and managing parking resources, the system can adapt to dynamic conditions and user behaviors, offering personalized and efficient services to drivers.

This chapter highlights the critical role of smart technologies in addressing urban challenges and sets the stage for further advancements in smart parking systems, paving the way for smarter, and more efficient, and sustainable cities.

Author details

Vesna Knights[1*], Olivera Petrovska[2] and Marija Prchkovska[2]

1 Faculty of Technology and Technical Science, University "St. Kliment Ohridski", Bitola, Republic of North Macedonia

2 Faculty of Technical Sciences, Mother Teresa University, Skopje, Republic of North Macedonia

*Address all correspondence to: vesna.knights@uklo.edu.mk

References

[1] Ashton K. That 'internet of things' thing. RFID Journal. Jun 22, 2009;**22**(7): 97-114

[2] Panetta K. Gartner top 10 strategic technology trends for 2018. Gartner [Internet]. 2017 Oct 3. Available from: https://www.gartner.com/en/newsroom/press-releases/2017-10-03-gartner-identifies-the-top-10-strategic-technology-trends-for-2018 [Accessed: August 12, 2024]

[3] Cisco. Cisco Annual Internet Report (2018–2023) White Paper [Internet]. Available from: https://www.cisco.com/c/en/us/solutions/collateral/executive-perspectives/annual-internet-report/white-paper-c11-741490.html [Accessed: August 12, 2024]

[4] Khanna A, Kaur S. Internet of Things (IoT), Applications and Challenges: A Comprehensive Review. Wireless Personal Communications. 2020;**114**:1687-1762. DOI: 10.1007/s11277-020-07446-4

[5] Khan S, Ali R, Baig Z, Erwin A. IoT-based smart parking: A review on technology, solution and research prospects. Journal of Advanced Transportation. 2018;**2018**:1-11. DOI: 10.1155/2018/4125085

[6] Fraifer M, Fernström M. Investigation of smart parking systems and their technologies. Thirty Seventh International Conference on Information Systems. Dublin, Ireland: IoT Smart City Challenges Applications (ISCA 2016); Dec 9, 2016. p. 1-14

[7] Rao RM, Lambat M, Kapare S, Vidhate AP. Smart parking system using machine learning and Internet of Things. International Journal for Research in Applied Science and Engineering Technology. 2021;**9**(1):682. DOI: 10.22214/ijraset.2021.32904. Available from: https://www.ijraset.com/fileserve.php?FID=32904

[8] Sarker IH. Machine learning: Algorithms, real-world applications and research directions. SN Computer Science. 2021;**2**(3):1-21. DOI: 10.1007/s42979-021-00592-x

[9] Zhang Y, Lai Z, Sun H, Dong Z. A survey on smart parking: Solutions and technologies. IEEE Transactions on Industrial Informatics. 2017;**13**(4): 1529-1539. DOI: 10.1109/TII.2016.2611588

[10] Liu C, Fan H, Chen X. Wireless sensor networks in smart parking systems. Sensors. 2019;**19**(4):882. DOI: 10.3390/s19040882

[11] Chen W, Wu X, Ji J, He Q. Computer vision techniques for smart parking: A survey. IEEE Access. 2019;**7**: 178327-178344. DOI: 10.1109/ACCESS.2019.2958552

[12] Ochieng WY, Sauer K. Urban road user charging and its interaction with intelligent transport systems. IEE Proceedings - Intelligent Transport Systems. 2002;**149**(3):178-184. DOI: 10.1049/ip-its:20020523

[13] Biyik C, Allam Z, Pieri G, Moroni D, O'Fraifer M, O'Connell E, et al. Smart parking systems: Reviewing the literature, architecture and ways forward. Smart Cities. 2021;**4**: 623-642. DOI: 10.3390/smartcities 4020032

[14] Watene G, Musiega D, Ndegwa C. A GIS based parking management and dissemination system. International Journal of Scientific Research. 2013;**2**(7): 194-201. Available from: https://www.

academia.edu/78264477/A_GIS_Based_Parking_Management_and_Dissemination_Syste

[15] Aloi G, Caliciuri G, Fortino G, Gravina R, Pace P, Russo W, et al. Enabling IoT-based smart cities: A review. Wireless Personal Communications. 2016;**87**(4):1257-1276. DOI: 10.1007/s11277-015-2981-5

[16] Bakıcı T, Almirall E, Wareham J. A smart city initiative: The case of Barcelona. Journal of the Knowledge Economy. 2013;**4**:135-148. DOI: 10.1007/s13132-012-0084-9

[17] Tomàs M. The smart city and urban governance: The urban transformation of Barcelona, 2011–2023. Urban Research and Practice. 2023:1-18. Available from: https://www.tandfonline.com/doi/full/10.1080/17535069.2023.2277205. DOI: 10.1080/17535069.2023.2277205

[18] Barcelona Smart City Project [Internet]. Available from: https://ajuntament.barcelona.cat/digital/en. [Accessed: August 11, 2024]

[19] Abbas Q, Ahmad G, Alyas T, Alghamdi T, Alsaawy Y, Alzahrani A. Revolutionizing urban mobility: IoT-enhanced autonomous parking solutions with transfer learning for smart cities. Sensors. 2023;**23**(21):8753. DOI: 10.3390/s23218753

[20] SFpark Project, San Francisco. Available from: https://sfpark.org

[21] SFMTA.com/ParkingRates. Available from: https://www.sfmta.com/demand-responsive-parking-pricing

[22] Lee J, Babcock J, Pham TS, Bui TH, Kang M. Smart city as a social transition towards inclusive development through technology: A tale of four smart cities. International Journal of Urban Sciences. 2022;**27**(suppl. 1):75-100. DOI: 10.1080/12265934.2022.2074076

[23] Amsterdam Smart City. Available from: https://amsterdamsmartcity.com

[24] Joo YM. Developmentalist smart cities? The cases of Singapore and Seoul. International Journal of Urban Sciences. 2021;**27**(sup1):164-182. DOI: 10.1080/12265934.2021.1925143

[25] Srikanth AD, Schroepfer T. Network science-based analysis of urban green spaces in Singapore. International Journal on Smart and Sustainable Cities. 2023;**1**(1):2340004. DOI: 10.1142/S2972426023400044

[26] Singapore Smart Nation. Available from: https://www.smartnation.gov.sg

[27] Tekin H, Dikmen I. Inclusive smart cities: An exploratory study on the London smart city strategy. Buildings. 2024;**14**(2):485. DOI: 10.3390/buildings14020485

[28] Narkhede N, Khan S. Smart parking system using machine learning algorithms. International Journal of Advanced Research in Computer and Communication Engineering. 2020;**9**(3):1-6. DOI: 10.17148/IJARCCE.2020.9321

[29] Raj A, Shetty SD. Smart parking systems technologies, tools, and challenges for implementing in a smart city environment: A survey based on IoT & ML perspective. International Journal of Machine Learning and Cybernetics. 2024;**15**(7):1-22. DOI: 10.1007/s13042-023-02056-5

[30] Singh T, Rathore R, Gupta K, Vijay E, Harikrishnan R. Artificial intelligence-enabled smart parking system. In: Shaw RN, Siano P, Makhilef S, Ghosh A, Shimi SL, editors.

Innovations in Electrical and Electronic Engineering. ICEEE 2023. Lecture Notes in Electrical Engineering. Vol. 1115. Singapore: Springer; 2024. pp. 31-44. DOI: 10.1007/978-981-99-8661-3_31

[31] Knights VA, Gacovski Z, Deskovski S. Guidance and control system for platoon of autonomous mobile robots. Journal of Electrical Engineering. 2018;**6**:281-288. DOI: 10.17265/2328-2223/2018.05.005

[32] Antoska-Knights V, Gacovski Z, Deskovski S. Obstacles avoidance algorithm for mobile robots, using the potential fields method. Universal Journal of Electrical and Electronic Engineering. 2017;**5**(4):75-84. DOI: 10.13189/ujeee.2017.050402

[33] Knights V, Petrovska O. Dynamic modeling and simulation of mobile robot under disturbances and obstacles in an environment. Journal of Applied Mathematics and Computing. 2024;**8**(1): 59-67. DOI: 10.26855/jamc.2024.03.007

[34] Antoska V, Jovanović K, Petrović VM, Baščarević N, Stankovski M. Balance analysis of the mobile anthropomimetic robot under disturbances – ZMP approach. International Journal of Advanced Robotic Systems. 2013;**10**(4):1-10. DOI: 10.5772/56238

[35] Chataut R, Phoummalayvane A, Akl R. Unleashing the power of IoT: A comprehensive review of IoT applications and future prospects in healthcare, agriculture, smart homes, smart cities, and industry 4.0. Sensors. 2023;**23**:7194. DOI: 10.3390/s23167194

[36] Knights VA, Gacovski Z. Methods for detection and prevention of vulnerabilities in the IoT (internet of things) systems. In: Internet of Things - New Insights. London, UK: IntechOpen; 2024. DOI: 10.5772/intechopen.113898

[37] Tang J, Wan L, Schooling J, Zhao P, Chen J, Wei S. Automatic number plate recognition (ANPR) in smart cities: A systematic review on technological advancements and application cases. Cities. 2022;**129**:103833. DOI: 10.1016/j.cities.2022.103833

[38] Lubna MN, Shah SAA. Automatic number plate recognition: A detailed survey of relevant algorithms. Sensors. 2021;**21**:3028. DOI: 10.3390/s21093028

[39] Tripathi S, Shetty S, Jain S, Sharma V. Automatic Number Plate Recognition System (ANPR): The Implementation. The International Journal of Innovative Technology and Exploring Engineering (IJITEE). Jun 2021;**10**(8):1-5. ISSN: 2278-3075

[40] Sheng NW, Wan Muda WM, Annuar AZ, Wan Hassan WH. Parking system using radio-frequency identification (RFID) technology. In: Yacob NA, Tholibon DA, Mohd Yunus NY, Jamil Z, Mohd Tahir S, editors. Fundamental and Applied Sciences in Asia. Singapore: Springer; 2022. p. 49-54. DOI: 10.1007/978-981-19-4910-4_8

[41] Gupta A, Srivastava A, Anand R, Chawla P. IoT based smart vehicle parking system using RFID. The International Journal for Modern Trends in Science and Technology. 2021;**10**(2): 49-54

[42] Santoso H, Wibowo A, Sari R. Smart parking management system: An integration of RFID, ALPR, and WSN. International Journal of Computers and Applications. 2018;**179**(38):1-6

[43] Elfaki AO, Messoudi W, Bushnag A, Abuzneid S, Alhmiedat T. A smart real-time parking control and monitoring system. Sensors. 2023;**23**(24):9741. DOI: 10.3390/s23249741

[44] Vink JP, de Haan G. Comparison of machine learning techniques for target detection. Artificial Intelligence Review. 2015;**43**:125-139. DOI: 10.1007/s10462-012-9366-7

[45] Sarker IH. Machine learning: Algorithms, real-world applications and research directions. SN Computer Science. 2021;**2**(160):1-21. DOI: 10.1007/s42979-021-00592-x

[46] Boukerche A, Wang J. Machine learning-based traffic prediction models for intelligent transportation systems. Computer Networks. 2020;**181**:107495. DOI: 10.1016/j.comnet.2020.107495

[47] Pasala KL, Nathanail EG, Gavanas N, Adamos G, editors. Smart parking system (SPS): An intelligent image-processing based parking solution. In: Smart Energy for Smart Transport. CSUM 2022. Lecture Notes in Intelligent Transportation and Infrastructure. Cham: Springer; 2023. DOI: 10.1007/978-3-031-23721-8_25

[48] Mekni M, Atilho S, Greenfield B, Placzek B, Nassar M. Real-time smart parking integration in intelligent transportation systems (ITS). In: Arai K, editor. Proceedings of the Future Technologies Conference (FTC) 2023. Vol. 3. FTC 2023. Lecture Notes in Networks and Systems, Vol. 815. Cham: Springer; 2023. DOI: 10.1007/978-3-031-47457-6_14

[49] Wang Q, Zhan J, Ouyang X, Ren Y. SPS and DPS: Two new grid-based source location privacy protection schemes in wireless sensor networks. Sensors. 2019;**19**(9):2074. DOI: 10.3390/s19092074

[50] Bharadwaj M, Mahalakshmi S, Hegde VN. Work-in-progress: 'ParKnow'—A system for smart parking management. In: Auer M, Ram BK, editors. Cyber-Physical Systems and Digital Twins. REV2019 2019. Lecture Notes in Networks and Systems. Vol. 80. Cham: Springer; 2020. DOI: 10.1007/978-3-030-23162-0_23

[51] Sadeghzadeh N, Farajzadeh N, Dattatri N, et al. SPS vision net: Measuring sensory processing sensitivity via an artificial neural network. Cognitive Computation. 2024;**16**:1379-1392. DOI: 10.1007/s12559-023-10216-6

[52] Nam SM, Kim HJ. WSN-SES/MB: System entity structure and model base framework for large-scale wireless sensor networks. Sensors. 2021;**21**(2):430. DOI: 10.3390/s21020430

[53] Ilhan A, Fietkiewicz KJ, Stock WG. Do car drivers really need mobile parking payment? In: Marcus A, Wang W, editors. Design, User Experience, and Usability: Designing Pleasurable Experiences. DUXU 2017. Lecture Notes in Computer Science. Vol. 10289. Cham: Springer; 2017. DOI: 10.1007/978-3-319-58637-3_19

Chapter 3

Fusion of Blockchain and Machine Learning: A Case of Secure Smart Grid

Samuel W. Kibret

Abstract

The Internet of Things (IoT) is a rapidly growing field that provides advanced solutions in various domains, including critical infrastructures. With the help of IoT, the traditional power system network can be transformed into a more effective and smarter (energy) grid. However, the security vulnerabilities related to IoT technologies have become a major concern for IoT-enabled energy systems. In this chapter, we will review the architecture and functionalities of IoT-enabled Smart Grid systems. Additionally, we will assess the underlying security vulnerabilities and develop a security solution that combines blockchain and machine learning to ensure system resilience and security. We will also conduct performance measurements of communication, computation, memory, and energy requirements while proposing mitigation techniques for Distributed Denial of Service (DoS) attacks.

Keywords: energy grid security, federated learning, remote attestation, distributed systems, blockchain

1. Introduction

An embedded device is generally characterized by its limited hardware resources, such as CPU power, RAM memory, and GPU power. These devices are typically embedded into other objects to serve a specific purpose. In today's interconnected computing systems, these devices form a network of interconnected objects over the internet, often referred to as the Internet of Things (IoT) [1].

The term Cyber-Physical Systems (CPS) and Industrial Internet of Things (IIoTs) refers to systems that consist of numerous interconnected components in a network. These systems are used in critical applications such as Smart Grids, process control, robotics, and nuclear reactors. The terms IIoTs and CPS are closely related and are often used interchangeably. According to a recent Gartner report, there were over 25 billion Internet of Things (IoT) devices in 2021, and this number is projected to increase to 75 billion by the end of 2025 [2].

A Smart Grid [3, 4] is an advanced power system that can automate and manage the growing complexity and demands of electricity. Smart Grids utilize digital communication technology and sensors to optimize the generation, transmission, and distribution of electricity. This power distribution infrastructure provides two-way communication between utility providers and customers. However, the communication networks in the Smart Grid bring increased connectivity, along with more severe security vulnerabilities and challenges. The Smart Grid is a prime target for cyber-attacks due to its critical nature. Consequently, Smart Grid security is receiving significant attention from governments, energy industries, and consumers.

1.1 Related work

Various types of cyber-attacks have shown that smart power systems are vulnerable to different threats. Attacks on industrial energy networks have fundamentally changed the view of the security of these systems. Recent studies have revealed that a vast number of attacks are injected as malware [5–8], affecting the integrity of the software running on the devices as well as the underlying system's firmware. Stuxnet [8] is considered the first known attack on industrial networks. The worm used a zero-day attack, a vulnerability that had not yet been discovered by a hardware or software manufacturer at the time of the attack, giving the attacker a significant advantage. This worm was programmed to target industrial power networks and was as sophisticated as it could hide itself in the system, making it appear to function correctly.

Operation Night Dragon [9] is another attack on the security of distribution network cells that can access both external and internal networks through techniques such as SQL injection, brute-force attack, phishing, or social engineering. These methods enable attackers to gain control over target devices and upload codes designed to administer the network and devices. On the other hand, the Shamoon Virus [10] targeted users of Microsoft Windows NT stations in industrial networks and caused devastating damage by deleting stored data. The BlackEnergy [11] malware is yet another attack on power grids, successfully infiltrating a smart energy distribution network through phishing emails sent to employees of the Ukrainian power grid company. Once the attackers gained control of the computer inside the power plant, they attacked the SCADA infrastructure, turning off as many devices as possible.

Further, there have been instances of attacks on nuclear power plants using large-scale DDoS attacks employing IoT botnets like Mirai and Hajime [12, 13]. There is also the potential for disruption of power grids using high-wattage devices [14], as well as the spread of malware citywide through deployed Phillips Hue bulbs, underscoring the importance of ensuring the security of these networks and their ability to recover quickly and cost-effectively from such attacks [15].

1.2 Contributions

In this chapter, we introduce a machine learning-based security solution for the Smart Grid. This blockchain-enabled approach offers various advantages over other security solutions. It is transparent, decentralized, has no single point of failure (SPoF), and addresses both static and runtime attacks (**Table 1**).

In IoTs, devices work together as a group [17]. However, SWATT [16] and C-FLAT [18] only support attestation of one device at a time. These techniques are impractical when dealing with a swarm of multiple devices that need to be connected in order to collaborate for security-sensitive processes. On the other hand, assuming a single central verifier makes swarm attestation scalable, but it is highly inefficient in terms of runtime cost. Additionally, this approach does not allow for topology changes, meaning that the network topology must remain static for the entire

	Scalable	Security support	Verification scheme	What (property) to verify?	Approach	Supported topology
SWATT [16]	No	Trusted Software	Centralized	Static	Traditional	Static
SEDA [17]	Yes	Hybrid	Centralized	Static	Traditional	Static
C-FLAT [18]	No	Hybrid	Centralized	Runtime	Traditional	Static
PADS [19]	Yes	Hybrid	Distributed	Static	Traditional	Static
DADS [20]	Yes	Hybrid	Decentralized	Static	Traditional	Dynamic
Airmed [21]	Yes	Hybrid	Decentralized	Static	Traditional	Dynamic
Energy management in smart grid [22]	Yes	Other	Centralized	Runtime	ML-based	Dynamic
AI-powered security for IoT [23]	Yes	Hybrid	Decentralized	Both	ML-based	Dynamic
This work	Yes	Hybrid	Decentralized	Both	ML-based	Dynamic

Table 1.
Features offered by different verification schemes (device swarm perspective).

attestation session. Moreover, this method is vulnerable to a SPoF. Decentralizing the verifier's duties among collaborating devices would increase swarm attestation efficiency and improve network resiliency [20, 21].

On the other hand, PADS [19], which is based on a non-interactive attestation scheme, is an innovative work that addresses highly dynamic networks. This work enables swarm attestation in a network of mobile IoT devices with an unstructured topology. PADS simplifies the attestation problem by finding a minimum consensus and computes attestation in a distributed manner.

When it comes to security support, the software-based approach [16] depends on difficult assumptions such as accurately estimating the round-trip time between the prover and verifier, and the optimality of the attestation algorithm, which are challenging to achieve [24]. The hardware-based approach [25], on the other hand, offers strong security assurances, but it is complex and costly for low-end embedded devices. Conversely, hybrid attestation techniques incur minimal hardware costs.

Except for C-FLAT [18], energy management in Smart Grid [22], AI-powered security for IoT [23], and the proposed approach, all existing attestation schemes focus on verifying the integrity of the binary code loaded in the device's memory. However, they are static in nature and do not cover runtime attacks, making member devices susceptible to such attacks. It is important to attest both the static and runtime properties for comprehensive security.

When we consider the verification methods employed, all attestation schemes except for Energy management in Smart Grids, AI-powered security for IoT, and the proposed approaches utilize the traditional remote attestation approach where the attestation measurement entity checks the underlying attestable memory property. Integrating Machine Learning techniques [22, 23] into security assurance methods could streamline the entire service delivery process, enhance efficiency, and guarantee system security and resilience.

2. Problem definition, attack model, and assumptions

We are considering software-only attacks, meaning remote and local adversaries cannot physically tamper with devices in the swarm.

An adversary may launch various attacks and modify the software configuration of the untrusted device (prover). Additionally, a local adversary may position itself close enough to the prover to eavesdrop and manipulate its communication channels [26]. This implies that, apart from attempting to compromise a target device, an adversary can also carry out active and passive attacks on the messages being communicated. Passive attacks aim to learn and use the system's information without affecting the system resources. The target of the attack is solely the transmitted information, in order to learn the system's configuration, architecture, and normal operational behavior. In general, an adversary could compromise the software configuration of the target device, forge messages between communicating devices, and alter the runtime behavior of the running code without changing its binary.

3. The proposed protocol

In the Internet of Things (IoT) and Cyber-Physical Systems (CPS), devices can form swarms and are interconnected. In the case of the Smart Grid, a large amount of individual energy data from local stations needs to be transferred to a central storage (such as the cloud or central power station). This exchange of data can lead to privacy violations and data misuse risks. To address this, we propose Federated Learning, where local stations collaborate to train a shared central model while keeping their energy data decentralized to preserve privacy and security. Following this, we employ a Blockchain-enabled approach to Smart Grid and energy exchange, where individual chains contain energy-related data and demand response (DR) transactions. These transactions involve taking explicit actions to reduce energy consumption in response to short-term high prices by local stations. The Distributed Ledger saves the transaction history and can also transparently accommodate the addition of new data from existing or new local stations.

Smart Grids: All electricity grids are networks that deliver electricity from power generation sources (power plants) to end-users such as businesses, factories, and homes. These systems enable electricity to be shared across long distances through a network of transmission lines.

A Smart Grid [4] performs all the functions of a traditional electricity grid. It also serves as a communication channel between electricity suppliers and users, using sensing and monitoring technology to transfer data throughout the grid. The concept of a Smart Grid is evolving to integrate distributed energy sources (DES), renewable energy sources (RES), and electric vehicles (EVs) into the power network. By employing various smart technologies, it creates a more adaptable and trustworthy grid. Smart Grids not only transmit electricity but also information, which is essential for managing energy systems. Therefore, they are centered around data monitoring, measuring, sharing, and acting on information. Smart Grid technologies include smart meters (for monitoring usage in real-time), phasor measurement units (PMUs) to monitor fluctuations in voltage or current to protect electrical appliances, and digital protective relays to safeguard the network in case of malfunctions.

3.1 Remote attestation

Remote attestation (RA) (see **Figure 1**) involves providing a status report of a device to a trusted party to demonstrate that it is functioning according to the specifications. It is important to note that the proposed approach verifies both the runtime and static behaviors of the target program. To maintain these features, we use the same approach as [23, 27], where the application program running in the local power station is attested against its execution (runtime) properties.

We use the *k-nearest neighbors* (a nonparametric supervised) algorithm to classify how individual execution time data is grouped. It is worth noting that the algorithm is a simple, easy-to-implement supervised machine learning algorithm that can be preferably used in IoTs. We use a K value of 5 to accurately predict outcomes. It is important to note that the number of optimal neighbors is $K = \sqrt{N}$, where N is the total number of points in the training dataset. We generally adopt the same approach as [23], where the prover—in our case, the target system or a Local Station (LS)—monitors every instruction of the running application program to evaluate the accuracy of the following execution time properties:

- number of *instructions*
- the number of CPU *cycles*
- number of *branch Instructions*
- number of *branch misses*
- number of *cache misses*
- the number of *hits* in the *last-level CPU cache* (both *loads* and *stores*).

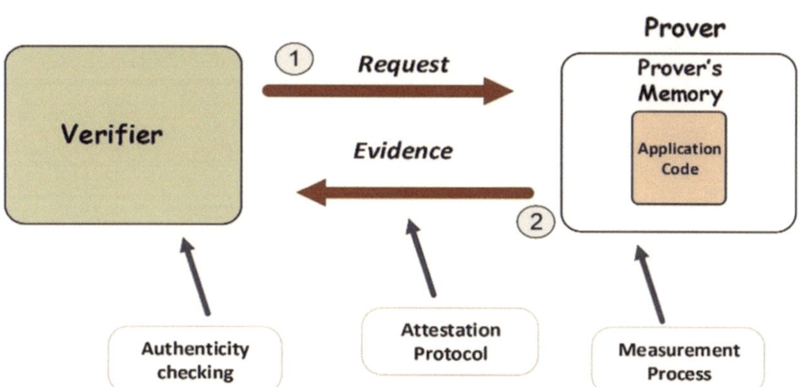

Figure 1.
Remote attestation.

3.2 Federated learning framework of the proposed solution

In Section 3.1, we discussed the verification of each member device's execution time properties. Genuine (attested) nodes are part of the group involved in Machine Learning (ML) model training. We use Federated Learning (FL) [28], also known as collaborative learning, a novel ML approach that trains ML models over various member local stations. These stations (devices or nodes) hold different local data and are placed at various locations. **Figure 2** illustrates the generic Smart Grid architecture and Federated Learning-enabled stations. Only ML model-related data of the local stations are shared with the Central server while keeping private and user data secure on the nodes. The nodes exchange shared parameters with the central server and perform training and evaluation of the ML models using their local data. The central server aggregates the parameters of the model from various nodes, enabling collaborative learning. Our FL platform supports the ML classifier over various decentralized nodes that hold the local data samples, enabling node-level prediction without sharing local private data.

As depicted in **Figure 2**, the local stations (nodes) are able to receive real-time energy usage data from smart meters in their vicinity. They also update DR data with other local stations, and securely communicate with the central server to exchange the parameters of the machine learning model. We use heterogeneous Federated Learning where member local stations may have different computation and communication capabilities. The idea is that the global inference model is trained from locally distributed data {**X1**, … , **Xn**} across ***n*** local stations.

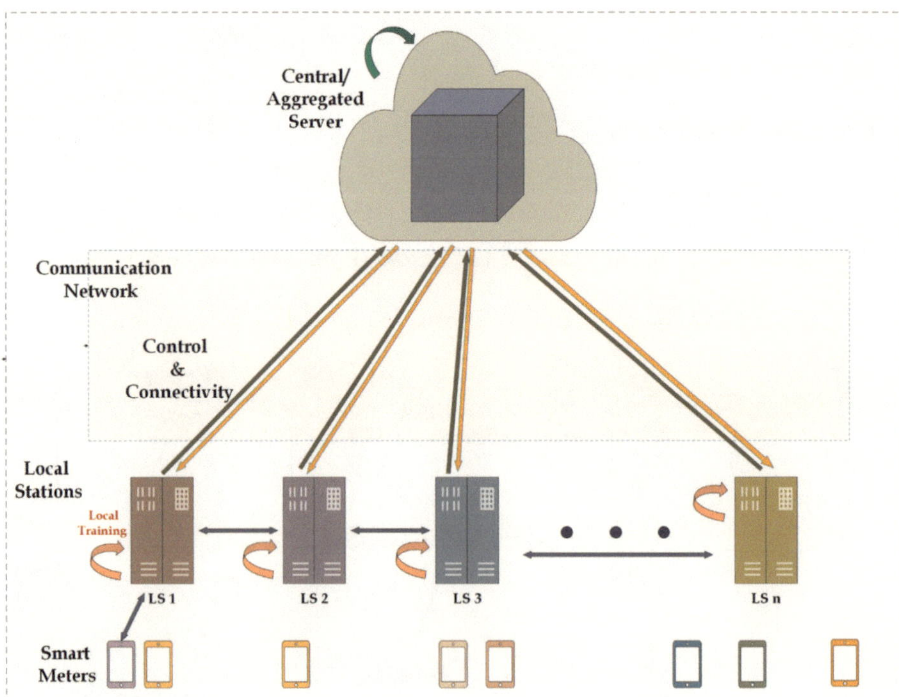

Figure 2.
Smart grid architecture and corresponding collaborative federated learning.

Upon training:

- The local stations retrieve machine learning parameters from the central server and evaluate them using their data. These local models are parameterized by model parameters **{W1, … , Wn}**.

- The central server is responsible for initializing the federated learning model by broadcasting default parameters to all local stations. It then receives the local parameters, aggregates them, and broadcasts the improved parameters back to the local stations. This activity is carried out multiple rounds and can be formulated as:

$$W_g^t = \frac{1}{n}\sum\nolimits_{i=0}^{n} W_i^t\,, \tag{1}$$

Where t is the number of iterations, n is total number of LS in the group, and W_g^t is the global model parameter after the tth iteration.

The pseudo-code for the proposed approach is shown in **Algorithm 1**.

Algorithm 1. Federated learning of the proposed approach.

Input: Data X_i distributed on N LS, the number of local Epochs E, local minibatch size B, learning rate η, global model parametrized by X_i, the number of computation complexity level C, number of iterations t, the channel shrinkage ratio r

Central server, ***CS***	Local station ***m***, LS_m

Initialize W_g^t, local capability information $L_{1:K}$
for each iteration t = 1, 2, 3, … , **do**
  $N_t \leftarrow 1$
  $S_t \leftarrow$ random set of N_t local stations
  for each local station n ∈ S_t **do**
    evaluate computation complexity level ***c*** from L_n
    m, r_m, W_m →	

	$B_m \leftarrow$ Split local data X_m into batches of size B
	for each local epoch e = 1, 2, 3, … , E **do**
	  for batch b_m ∈ B_m **do**
	    $W_m \leftarrow W_m - \eta\nabla l\,(W_m, r_m, b_m)$
	  end
	end
	Return W_m to *CS*

W_m^{t+1} ← m, r_m, W_m^t
  end
  for each computation complexity level c **do**
    perform global aggregation
  end
  $W_g^{t+1} \leftarrow$ aggregated value /*assign the global aggregated value to the next iteration of the global model parameter */
end
Query the local stations local running statistics
Update batch B statistics	

3.3 Blockchain-enabled P2P communication and energy data exchange

The blockchain (BC) [29] is a shared, digitized, distributed, and verifiable data store used in Bitcoin and other cryptocurrencies. Transactions are recorded chronologically and publicly. Some key features of a blockchain that make it well-suited for IoT, and more specifically Smart Grid, include decentralization, which ensures scalability and robustness by removing central control, and security achieved through a chain of trust. Member local stations exchange energy data as well as demand response-related information (transactions) with each other.

In a blockchain-based implementation, when a transaction occurs, the originating system (referred to as LS_G) creates the first block in the chain, known as the *Genesis block*. Each block contains the following information: ***LS*** identifier (***idLS***), transaction identifier (***idTrans***), hash digest resulting from the transaction, digest resulting from a previous execution, a timestamp, and the ***LS*** signature. Since the Genesis block has no predecessor, it only points to itself. When a second transaction occurs, the underlying ***LS*** verifies it. Upon successful verification, a new block containing the mentioned components is created and broadcasted. This creates a chain where each block references the previous one, all the way back to the genesis block (see **Figure 3** below). ***LSs*** utilizes the trained FL framework (the generated global inference model) to verify DR-related transactions and other energy-related data in the construction of chains.

4. Implementation and performance evaluation

We implement our protocol on the ARM TrustZone Architecture [30], which is designed to create a secure execution environment by dividing processing environments into two distinct worlds: *Normal* and *Secure*. These two environments have their own address spaces and different privileges. While *Secure World* can access the code and data present in the *Normal World*, its processing remains unaffected by anything that happens in the normal world. Our implementation can be equally applied to any embedded architecture with minimal hardware security, as provided by SMART [31] and TrustLite [32].

4.1 Performance evaluation

In Section 3.1, we discussed the use of the ***KNN*** algorithm for verifying member devices (***LSs***). For testing the classifier's accuracy, we utilized a real IoT application, specifically a soldering iron temperature controller [33]. The classifier relies on six features: the total number of *instructions*, *cycles*, *branch instructions*, *branch misses*, *cache misses*, and *cache references* for the underlying application (refer to Section 3.1).

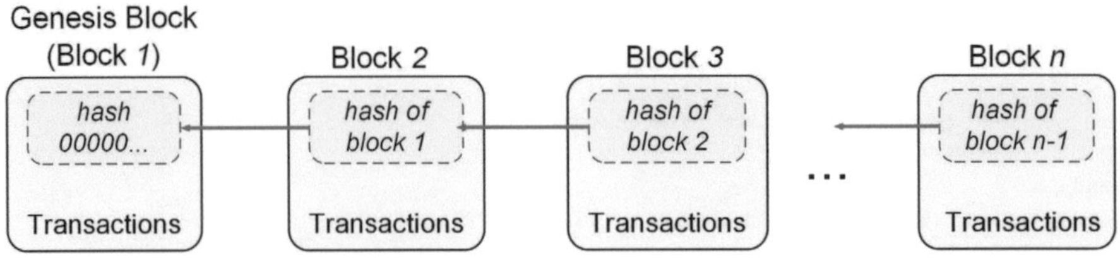

Figure 3.
Overview of the blockchain data structure.

Furthermore, we employed the common 80:20 train-test ratio to divide our data set into training and testing sets [34]. This means that 80% of the observations were used for training, while the remaining 20% were reserved for testing. The classifier demonstrated a strong verification rate of 99.6% and proved its robustness and ability to avoid false positives. It is worth noting that we utilized TensorFlow Federated (TFF) [35], an open-source framework for machine learning and other computations on decentralized data.

4.1.1 Performance of our approach for single device attestation

Figure 4 illustrates the runtime performance of the proposed approach. As depicted in the graph, the attestation overhead appears to be linear to the corresponding execution (runtime) events due to the context switch between the *Secure* and *Normal Worlds*.

Similar to [27], a single device experiment has been conducted on OP-TEE [36], an ARM TrustZone-based open-source implementation of TEE (Trusted Execution Environment). Additionally, communication has been secured with HMAC using SHA-1 [37] and signed with ECDSA [38].

a. *Computation cost*

   The most significant portion of the computation cost in our approach is attributed to cryptographic operations, specifically the creation/verification of digital signatures (σ) and the creation/verification of benign software configurations (*MACs*/*VERMACs*). Additionally, member devices also perform computations for creating/verifying blocks.

b. *Communication cost*

   Communication cost depends on the volume of data transferred between devices, which is determined by the number of communicating devices and their descendants.

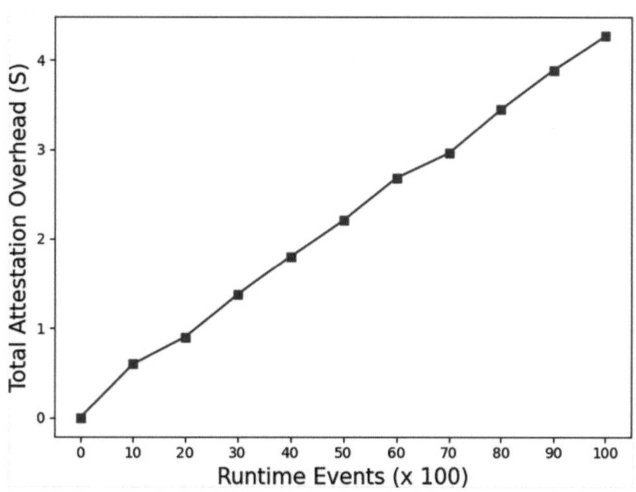

Figure 4.
Single device (local station) attestation of the proposed approach.

c. *Memory requirements*

In the new scheme, each ***LS*** stores Local Station identifiers ($\boldsymbol{idLS_i}, \ldots, \boldsymbol{idLS_n}$) in its communication network, along with a signing keypair ($\boldsymbol{sK_i}, \boldsymbol{pK_i}$), identity certificate cert($\boldsymbol{pK_i}$), code certificate cert(ci), a set of attestation keys *K* shared with its neighbors in the network, and one session identifier *sn* for the duration of each block instance.

d. *Energy cost*

Energy is essentially required for sending/receiving a message, generating a random number, and computing *MAC*/*VERMAC* and digital signatures (σ). Let the energy required to send one byte be E_{send}, to receive one byte be E_{recv}, to generate a random number (i.e., 20 random bytes) be E_{prng}, to compute *MAC*/*VERMAC* be E_{mac}, and to sign be E_{sign}.

e. *Security analysis*

The proposed approach aims to enable secure detection through remote attestation and ensure that a chain is formed in the *Blockchain* among genuine devices in a network, where their execution time properties are the same. It is important to note that our adversarial model only considers remote and local adversaries (see Section 2.1), while physical attacks are not within the scope.

Due to the preimage and collision resistance nature of *MAC*, we utilize *MAC* as *HMAC*. The probability that Adversary *A* forges verification reports is negligible in l_{mac}. In the case of attestation report forgery, *A* would need to know the pair-wise attestation key K_{XZ} or forge the hashed Verification report to cause any kind of modification, where ***X*** and ***Z*** are the two communicating ***LSs***. However, neither case is feasible in light of the key storage and *MAC* features discussed above.

The verification code execution is isolated from the rest of the system (see Section 4). Verification code executions take place in the *Secure World*, where they are protected from other processes in the *Normal World*. This means that any changes in the operating system do not affect the functionality of the measurement entity.

Our approach also helps to mitigate *DoS* (Denial-of-Service) attacks by maintaining a record of the number of fake messages received from a particular ***LS***. If the number of fake messages exceeds a certain value, we take action. Generally, a *DoS* attack is not severe because it does not cause any computation on other ***LSs***.

4.1.2 *Performance of the proposed federated learning*

In the case of the proposed federated learning, the performance of the approach depends on the capability of the ***LSs***. We assume that the ***LSs*** have sufficient hardware to run the model.

As outlined in Algorithm 1 above, during each round, only a subset of ***LSs*** train the model. We adjust the number of clients in the subset selected in each round to observe the impact of larger subsets. Additionally, we vary the number of epochs of local training. In all scenarios, the federated learning algorithm was executed for 10 rounds.

Figure 5(a) and **(b)** show the actual and predicted profiles for the soldering iron temperature controller application after 5 and 20 epochs, where an epoch represents a complete pass of our training dataset through the learning algorithm we developed.

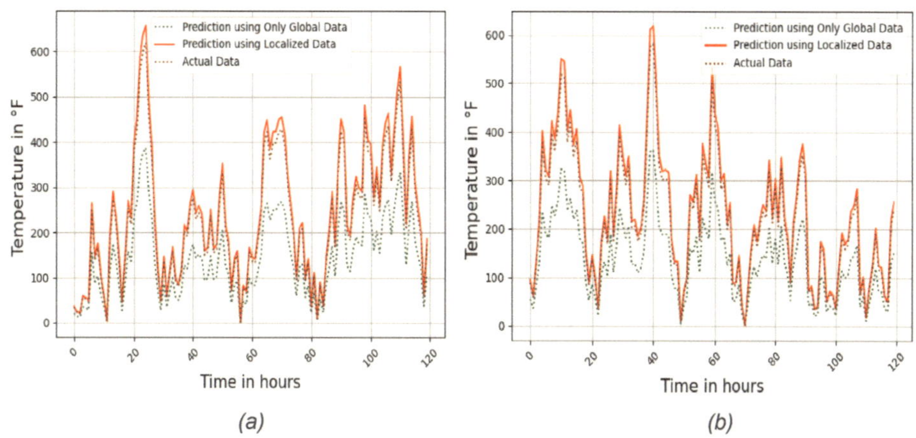

Figure 5.
Temperature predictions over time for a LS.

As shown in the figures, our method effectively trains the model using a specific subset of LSs as described in **Algorithm 1** above. Sufficient local data enables the approach to generate more accurate results.

5. Conclusion

In this chapter, we introduced a Federated Learning Framework designed to address security issues in a Smart Grid. Each member device (local station) is verified for the execution time behaviors of the underlying running program. This approach enables the local stations to tackle both static and runtime attacks. These verified members then collaborate to train the ML model. Our approach facilitates accurate on-device predictions for energy data and demand response-related transactions among member local stations in Smart Grids. This contributes to creating transparent, robust, and secure chains of blocks. We evaluated and demonstrated the feasibility of our approach on ARM TrustZone security extensions for embedded devices. Performance evaluations of our approach indicate that the proposed technique yields promising results.

Acronyms

BC	blockchain
CPS	cyber-physical systems
CS	central server
DDoS	distributed denial-of-service
DES	distributed energy sources
DoS	Denial-of-service
DR	demand response
ECDSA	elliptic curve digital signature algorithm
EV	electric vehicle
FL	federated learning

IIoT	industrial Internet of Things
IoT	Internet of Things
KNN	k-nearest neighbors
LS	local station
MAC	message authentication code
ML	machine learning
OP-TEE	open-source trusted execution environment
PMU	phasor measurement units
P2P	peer-to-peer
RA	remote attestation
RES	renewable energy sources
SHA	Secure Hash Algorithm
SPoF	single point of failure
SQL	structured query language
TEE	trusted execution environment
TFF	TensorFlow Federated
VERMAC	verify message authentication code

Author details

Samuel W. Kibret[1,2]

1 Indian Institute of Technology Delhi, India

2 Independent Researcher, Rockville, MD, USA

*Address all correspondence to: samuel_wed@yahoo.com; samuel.wed@cse.iitd.ac.in

References

[1] Kibret SW. Decentralized Mechanisms to Attest Recover and Update IoT Networks. New Delhi, Delhi, India: IIT Delhi; 2022. Available from: http://hdl.handle.net/10603/441308

[2] Gartner says a thirty-fold increase in internet-connected physical devices by 2020 will significantly alter how the supply chain operates. 2019. Available from: http://www.gartner.com/newsroom/id/2688717

[3] Kim S-K, Huh J-H. A study on the improvement of smart grid security performance and blockchain smart grid perspective. Energies. 2018;**11**:1973. DOI: 10.3390/en11081973

[4] Smart grid explained. Blog. Available from: https://sympower.net/smart-grid-explained/

[5] Illera AG, Vidal JV. Lights off! The Darkness of the Smart Meters. Europe: BlackHat; 2014

[6] Kabay M. Attacks on Power Systems: Hackers Malware. Boston, Massachusetts, USA: Norwich University; 2010. Available from: https://www.networkworld.com/article/2217684/attacks-on-power-systems–hackers–malware.html [Accessed: September 12, 2024]

[7] Pollet J, Cummins J. Electricity for free? The dirty underbelly of scada and smart meters. In: Proceedings of Black Hat USA, 2010. 2010. Availabe from: https://infocondb.org/con/black-hat/black-hat-usa-2010/electricity-for-free-the-dirty-underbelly-of-scada-and-smart-meters

[8] Vijayan J. Stuxnet Renews Power Grid Security Concerns. Vol. 26. Framingham, Massachusetts, USA: Computerworld; 2010. Available from: https://www.computerworld.com/article/2519574/stuxnet-renews-power-grid-security-concerns.html [Accessed: September 12, 2024]

[9] Cyberattacks, Global Energy. Night dragon. In: McAfee Foundstone Professional Services and McAfee Labs. Santa Clara, CA, USA: McAfee, Inc.; 2011

[10] Bronk C, Tikk-Ringas E. The cyber attack on Saudi Aramco. Survival. 2013; **55**(2):81-96. DOI: 10.1080/00396338.2013.784468

[11] Main DLL. BlackEnergy & Quedagh. In: Proceedings of the 2017 International Conference on Cyber Security and Protection of Digital Services. Piscataway, NJ, USA: IEEE; 2017

[12] Antonakakis M, April T, Bailey M, Bernhard M, Bursztein E, Cochran J, et al. Understanding the mirai botnet. In: 26th USENIX Security Symposium (USENIX Security 17). Berkeley, CA, USA: USENIX Association; 2017. pp. 1093-1110

[13] Kolias C, Kambourakis G, Stavrou A, Voas J. DDoS in the IoT: Mirai and other botnets. Computer. 2017;**50**(7):80-84

[14] Soltan S, Mittal P, Poor HV. Blackiot: IoT botnet of high wattage devices can disrupt the power grid. In: 27th USENIX Security Symposium (USENIX Security 18). Berkeley, CA, USA: USENIX Association; 2018. pp. 15-32

[15] Ronen E, Shamir A, Weingarten A-O, O'Flynn C. IoT goes nuclear: Creating a zigbee chain reaction. In: 2017 IEEE Symposium on Security and Privacy

(SP). Piscataway, New Jersey, USA: IEEE; 2017. pp. 195-212

[16] Seshadri A, Perrig A, Van Doorn L, Khosla P. Swatt: Softwar based attestation for embedded devices. In: Null. Piscataway, New Jersey, USA: IEEE; 2004. p. 272

[17] Asokan N, Brasser F, Ibrahim A, Sadeghi A-R, Schunter M, Tsudik G, et al. Seda: Scalable embedded device attestation. In: Proceedings of the 22nd ACM SIGSAC Conference on Computer and Communications Security. New York, NY, USA: ACM; 2015. pp. 964-975

[18] Tigist A, Asokan N, Davi L, Ekberg J-E, Nyman T, Paverd A, et al. C-flat: Control-flow attestation for embedded systems software. In: Proceedings of the 2016 ACM SIGSAC Conference on Computer and Communications Security. New York, NY, USA: ACM; 2016. pp. 743-754

[19] Ambrosin M, Conti M, Riccardo Lazzeretti M, Rabbani M, Ranise S. Pads: Practical attestation for highly dynamic swarm topologies. In: 2018 International Workshop on Secure Internet of Things (SIoT). Piscataway, NJ, USA: IEEE; 2018. pp. 18-27

[20] Wedaj S, Paul K, Ribeiro VJ. Dads: Decentralized attestation for deviceswarms. ACM Transactions on Privacy and Security (TOPS). 2019; **22**(3):19. DOI: 10.1145/3325822

[21] Sourav D, Wedaj S, Paul K, Bellur U, Ribeiro VJ. Airmed: Efficient self-healing network of low-end devices. arXivpreprint arXiv:2004.12442. 2020: 1-204. Available from: https://arxiv.org/abs/2004.12442

[22] Salinas S, Li M, Li P, Fu Y. Dynamic energy management for the smart grid with distributed energy resources. IEEE Transactions on Smart Grid. 2013;**4**(4): 2139-2151. DOI: 10.1109/TSG.2013.2265556

[23] Kibret SW, Paul K, Ribeiro VJ. AI-Powered Security for IoT: A Blockchain Enabled Device Twin Approach. London, UK: IntechOpen; 2023. DOI: 10.5772/intechopen.1003003

[24] Armknecht F, Sadeghi A-R, Schulz S, Wachsmann C. A security framework for the analysis and design of software attestation. In: Proceedings of the 2013 ACM SIGSAC Conference on Computer & Communications Security. New York, NY, USA: ACM; 2013. pp. 1-12. DOI: 10.1145/2508859.2516650

[25] Kong J, Koushanfar F, Pendyala PK, Sadeghi A-R, Chris tian Wachsmann. Pufatt: Embedded platform attestation based on novel processor-based pufs. In: 2014 51st ACM/EDAC/IEEE Design Automation Conference (DAC). Piscataway, NJ, USA: IEEE; 2014. pp. 1-6

[26] Dolev D, Yao A. On the security of public key protocols. IEEE Transactions on Information Theory. 1983;**29**(2):198-208. Available from: https://ieeexplore.ieee.org/stamp/stamp.jsp?arnumber=1056650

[27] Kibret SW. Property-Based Attestation in Device Swarms: A Machine Learning Approach. 2nd ed. Berlin, Boston: De Gruyter; 2023. pp. 71-90. DOI: 10.1007/3-540-09237-4

[28] Konečný J. Federated learning: Strategies for improving communication efficiency. 2016. arXiv preprint arXiv: 1610.05492. Available from: https://arxiv.org/pdf/1610.05492

[29] Nakamoto S et al. Bitcoin: A Peer-to-Peer Electronic Cash System. 2008

[30] ARM Holdings. Arm Security Technology: Building a Secure System

Using Trustzone Technology. Cambridge, United Kingdom: ARM Holdings; 2009. Available from: https://developer.arm.com/documentation/genc009492/latest

[31] Eldefrawy K, Tsudik G, Francillon A, Perito D. Smart: Secure and minimal architecture for (establishing dynamic) root of trust. In: NDSS. Vol. 12. Reston, VA, USA: The Internet Society; 2012. pp. 1-15

[32] Koeberl P, Schulz S, Sadeghi A-R, Varadharajan V. Trustlite: A security architecture for tiny embedded devices. In: Proceedings of the Ninth European Conference on Computer Systems. New York, NY, USA: ACM; 2014. p. 10

[33] Soldering Iron. Soldering Iron Controller for Hakko 907. Milan, Italy: Arduino; (n.d.). Available from: https://create.arduino.cc/projecthub/sfrwmaker/soldering-iron-controller-for-hakko-907-8c5866

[34] Joseph VR. Optimal ratio for data splitting. Statistical Analysis and Data Mining: The ASA Data Science Journal. 2022;**15**(4):531-538

[35] TensorFlow federated: Machine learning on decentralized data. Available from: https://www.tensorflow.org/federated [Accessed: March 08, 2024]

[36] OP-TEE. Open Source Implementation of TEE. OP-TEE; (n.d.). Available from: www.op-tee.org/

[37] Eastlake 3rd D, Jones P. US secure hash algorithm 1 (sha-1). Technical report. 2001. Available from: https://www.hjp.at/(st_a)/doc/rfc/rfc3174.html

[38] Johnson D, Menezes A, Vanstone S. The elliptic curve digital signature algorithm (ECDSA). International Journal of Information Security. 2001;**1**(1):36-63

Section 2

Smart Sensors and IoT

Chapter 4

Perspective Chapter: Unlocking the Potential of IoT in Education – Overcoming the Obstacles to Integration in Spanish Universities Using the Ishikawa Diagram

Nicoletta González-Cancelas, Alberto Camarero-Orive and Javier Vaca-Cabrero

Abstract

In the rapidly evolving educational landscape, a prime example is Spanish universities which have integrated Internet of Things (IoT) technologies aimed at redefining teaching and learning experiences. This chapter explores the current state of IoT adoption in Spanish universities, identifies the main challenges preventing its widespread implementation, and proposes strategic solutions. Key obstacles include inadequate technological infrastructure, lack of digital skills among faculty and students, and insufficient educational resources. Additionally, issues such as unrealistic expectations, resistance to change, and unclear legal frameworks further complicate integration efforts. Using the Ishikawa diagram, the research categorizes these barriers into four main groups: People, Processes, Infrastructure, and Educational Policies. Recommendations to overcome these challenges emphasize improving digital literacy, developing robust IoT-based pedagogical strategies, investing in modern infrastructure, and fostering a culture of innovation. The study concludes that a multidisciplinary and collaborative approach involving all stakeholders is essential for the successful integration of IoT in higher education.

Keywords: internet of things (IoT), Spanish universities, technological integration, educational innovation, digital literacy

1. Introduction

In today's dynamic educational landscape, Spanish universities are at a crucial juncture of transformation. Rapid technological evolution, driven by the Internet of Things (IoT) and Artificial Intelligence (AI), opens up an unprecedented range of possibilities to redefine teaching, learning, and the educational experience as a whole [1].

Spanish universities have a responsibility to take advantage of these emerging technologies to reimagine the education of the future.

The integration of IoT technologies in education promises to improve interactive learning, streamline administrative processes, and foster innovative research environments, adding many new opportunities to the education of the future.

As hubs of innovation and knowledge, Spanish universities have a responsibility to harness these emerging technologies to reimagine the education of the future. However, despite the enormous potential of IoT in education, its integration in Spanish universities faces several obstacles that must be overcome in order to unlock its full transformative potential [2].

Key challenges include inadequate technological infrastructure, a lack of digital skills among teachers and students, and insufficient educational resources. In addition, factors such as unrealistic expectations, resistance to change, and unclear legal frameworks further complicate integration efforts. These barriers hinder the full realization of the transformative potential of IoT in higher education [3].

This work aims to explore the current IoT landscape in Spanish university education, identify the main challenges that prevent its widespread adoption and propose strategic solutions to overcome these obstacles. The research uses the Ishikawa diagram, also known as the fishbone diagram, to categorize these barriers. By providing a comprehensive analysis of these issues, this study aims to contribute to the development of a strategic framework for the successful implementation of IoT in Spanish universities.

The ultimate goal is to highlight the need for a multidisciplinary and collaborative approach involving all stakeholders to achieve effective and sustainable IoT integration in higher education. In the case study, the main question is: What are the reasons that explain the lack of integration of IoT in the Spanish university educational environment as a tool to support teaching?

This chapter aims to explore the current landscape of IoT in Spanish university education, identify the main challenges preventing its widespread adoption, and propose strategies to overcome these obstacles. Through an in-depth analysis of the existing barriers, this chapter seeks to contribute to the creation of a strategic framework for the successful implementation of IoT in Spanish universities, allowing these institutions to take full advantage of the advantages offered by this disruptive technology.

This document is structured as follows: it reviews the current state of IoT adoption in education globally and in Spain. The main challenges identified are described below, categorized by the Ishikawa diagram. Strategic solutions and recommendations to overcome these challenges are presented. Finally, Section 5 concludes with a discussion of the implications of the results and suggestions for future research.

2. Challenges of Spanish university education

The current landscape of Spanish university education is at a turning point. On the one hand, there are signs of strength, such as the high enrolment rate, the quality of the institutions, and the relevance of research. However, they also face significant challenges that require profound transformation [4].

Educational technologies are a fundamental part of the strategy of all Spanish universities and can be considered critical to their mission [5].

The analysis of Spanish universities shows that there are educational technologies such as LMS, collaborative tools, videoconferencing, institutional content repositories, class recording systems, virtual laboratories or plagiarism detection tools that have a high degree of implementation, and others, such as makerspaces, micro-credentials, AI-based technologies, digital badges, etc. OER or VR/AR that are gradually growing and, finally, some that have experienced less attention or are not growing as expected such as MOOCs, SPOCs, IoT, or proctoring tools [6]. This information can be useful for strategic decision-making that seeks to position institutions in a certain place within the national panorama, either by achieving minimum or maximum objectives or by wanting to exploit one of the less exploited areas [7].

There are many challenges facing Spanish university education, among the most prominent is the lack of adaptation to the demands of the labor market due to the fact that the skills demanded in today's world do not always match those taught in universities, which generates a gap between academic training and the needs of the market [8].

In addition, traditional teaching methods focused on the transmission of knowledge and memorization, are not always effective for new generations of students and generate rigidity in teaching models [9].

Today's education does not always take into account the different needs, learning styles and rhythms of each student, with the insertion of new technologies the lack of personalization of learning can be alleviated [10].

Currently, there is a lack of exploitation of the potential of technologies, the integration of technologies in education is still incipient and their full potential to improve learning is not being exploited [11].

In this context, technological innovation is presented as a fundamental tool to address the challenges of Spanish university education and transform it into a more effective, efficient system adapted to the needs of the twenty-first century [12].

The use of IoT would bring benefits of technological innovation in university education, allowing, among other things—the personalization of learning since technologies allow learning to be adapted to the needs, learning styles, and rhythms of each student; greater interactivity and participation since technological tools encourage interaction between students, teachers, and content, making learning more dynamic and participatory; access to resources and experiences by enabling technologies to access a wide range of educational resources and experiences that are not always available in traditional settings; the assessment and monitoring of learning by facilitating continuous assessment and monitoring of student progress; and preparation for the world of work so that technologies help students develop the digital competencies and skills necessary for today's job market [4].

Technological innovation is an indispensable driver of change to transform Spanish university education and turn it into a system that prepares students for the challenges of the future [12].

The main impacts of IoT on university education can be grouped into three main blocks [13]:

- In learning: Describe how IoT can improve student learning by personalizing experiences, providing real-time feedback, and creating more immersive learning environments.

- In teaching: Explain how IoT can transform teaching practice, automate administrative tasks, facilitate collaboration, and provide new tools for assessing and tracking student progress.

- In institutional management: Analyze how IoT can optimize the management of universities, improving energy efficiency, security, and maintenance of facilities.

According to the CRUE's "Report on the Situation of Educational Technologies in Spanish Universities 2022", IoT technologies on university campuses can be used to measure temperature and humidity in a classroom, monitor air quality or the energy use of buildings, explore their potential to transform teaching, learning, and the overall educational experience. They can also be used to monitor lab usage or to track student attendance and participation in class. According to the data in its report, although these technologies are not yet integrated into our university campuses, as already anticipated in the 2017 Horizon Report, higher education institutions face uncertainty about the avalanche of smart devices in the coming years. As with the advent of Bring Your Own Device (BYOD), bandwidth needs must be considered and which devices are authorized to connect to campus networks must be determined.

The creation of "IoT Classrooms" will allow the generation of educational spaces equipped with sensors and smart devices that allow teachers to create more interactive and personalized learning experiences, in addition to creating educational spaces equipped with virtual and augmented reality that allows students to learn in a more experiential way. IoT can be used to improve campus security, accessibility, and sustainability [14].

As technology continues to evolve, expect more universities to embrace IoT to transform education and offer students more enriching and personalized learning experiences.

To determine the challenges faced by Spanish universities and what the use of IoT would entail, different methodologies such as the Delphi method, the Ishikawa diagram, surveys and questionnaires, in-depth interviews, focus groups with small groups of professors, students, and administrators can be used to discuss and explore in depth the barriers and facilitators of the IoT, PESTEL analysis, benchmarking, and other tools. With these tools, it will be possible to address the lack of integration of IoT in the Spanish university educational environment.

The use of these tools is based on several reasons. It has several reasons, the first of which is that they allow a comprehensive understanding of the problem, and a complete and detailed view of all the possible causes and factors that contribute to the lack of IoT integration. They also allow for the compilation of expert perspectives by engaging experts in technology, education, and other relevant fields to obtain high-quality qualitative and quantitative information. They not only identify the causes of the problem but also prioritize which ones have the greatest impact and need to be addressed first. They ensure that findings and recommendations are validated by stakeholders, ensuring their relevance and applicability. Fostering collaboration and participation of various stakeholders, promoting an inclusive and comprehensive approach, allows the problem to be addressed with a broader approach to reality.

The use of these methodologies is justified by their ability to provide a deep and structured understanding of complex problems such as the lack of IoT integration in university education. These methodologies allow for systematic information collection and analysis, involving experts and stakeholders, and developing effective, data-driven solutions. Ultimately, these tools facilitate a comprehensive and collaborative approach, crucial to addressing multifaceted challenges in the educational context.

3. Overcoming the obstacles to integration in Spanish universities using the Ishikawa diagram

The choice of the Ishikawa diagram to analyze the lack of IoT integration in Spanish universities is justified by its ability to break down complex problems into specific and categorized causes, providing a clear and structured visualization of the factors involved. It facilitates the identification of root causes and collaboration between various stakeholders, as well as being applicable in continuous improvement processes. This tool not only helps identify current issues but also serves as a basis for developing effective and detailed strategies to improve IoT adoption in the educational environment.

The methodological structure used to determine the reasons that explain the lack of integration of IoT in the Spanish university educational environment is described below. The hierarchical methodology provides a structured approach to use a Delphi panel in the creation of an Ishikawa diagram, allowing to identify in a systematic and consensual way the reasons that explain the lack of integration of IoT in the Spanish university educational environment. This approach facilitates a deep understanding of the problem and the formulation of effective strategies to address it.

1. Problem definition

    - Objective: To clearly establish the problem to be investigated.

    - Action: Formulate the central problem as: "Lack of integration of IoT in the Spanish university educational environment as a teaching support tool".

2. Delphi panel formation

    a. Criteria for selecting experts

        - Knowledge and experience: Experts in IoT technology, higher education, educational innovation, ICT applied to education.

        - Diversity: Experts from different universities and academic areas, as well as experts in emerging technologies.

        - Availability and commitment: Willingness to participate in several rounds of consultation.

3. Panel Delphi

    a. First round

        - Objective: To collect a wide range of reasons for the lack of IoT integration.

        - Action: Ask open-ended questions

b. Second and next rounds

- Analysis of responses from the first round: Group and categorize the answers obtained.

- Closed-ended questions: Formulate closed-ended questions for experts to evaluate and prioritize the reasons identified using a Likert scale.

- Consensus: Iteration and refinement, repeat the process until a consensus is reached.

4. Construction of the Ishikawa diagram

a. Main diagram categories

- Identification of main categories: Based on Delphi panel responses, such as methods, machinery, materials, labor, environment, and measurements.

b. Breakdown into secondary cases

- Subcategories: Break down each main category into secondary causes according to the information provided by the experts.

c. Diagram display

- Drawing the diagram: Graphically represent the central problem, main categories, and subcategories in the fishbone diagram.

5. Analysis of results and conclusions

- Data collection and analysis: Analyze the responses from each Delphi round to identify patterns and consensus.

6. Strategy development and implementation of results

- Strategy development: Use the results to develop strategies and policies that foster the integration of IoT into the university educational environment (**Figure 1**).

It is critical to have a clear understanding of the goals of the Delphi study. In this case, the objective is to identify and analyze the reasons that explain the lack of integration of IoT in the Spanish university educational environment.

Diagram, also known as a fishbone diagram or cause and effect diagram, is a very useful graphical tool for identifying and analyzing the possible causes of a problem or an unwanted effect. Its graphical representation facilitates the understanding and analysis of the different categories of causes that may be involved in a problem [15].

The diagram is made up of a main line that represents the problem or effect you want to analyze. From this main line, other lines branch out representing the different categories of possible causes. These categories typically include:

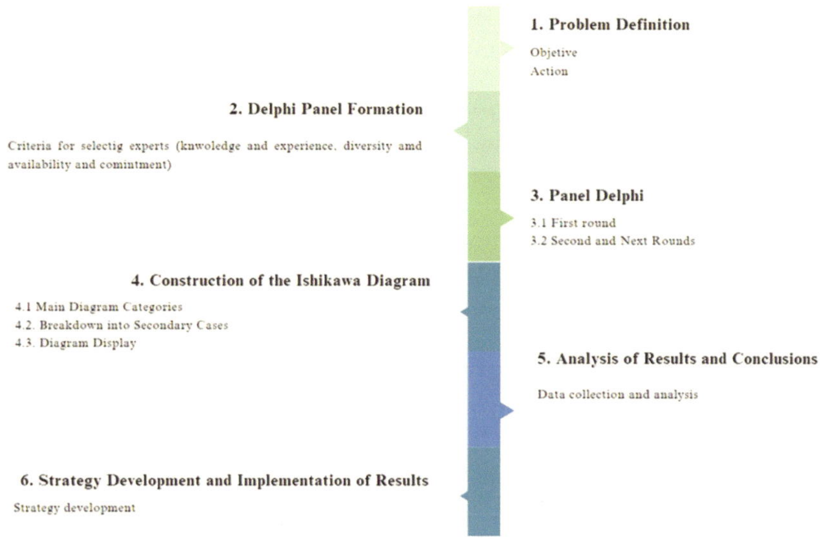

Figure 1.
Workflow for a Delphi panel. Source: own elaboration.

- Personnel: Factors related to the people working on the process, such as their experience, training, or motivation.

- Processes: The steps and activities that are carried out to produce a result.

- Materials: The resources and raw materials that are used in the process.

- Environment: The environmental conditions that can affect the process.

- Methods: The techniques and tools used to accomplish the work.

The benefits of the Ishikawa diagram are, among others, it facilitates the visualization of the causes of a problem, promotes creative thinking and brainstorming, helps identify the most relevant causes of a problem, and allows you to focus improvement efforts on the most critical areas.

The Ishikawa diagram is used in a wide variety of contexts, such as:

- Quality improvement: To identify the causes of quality problems and develop solutions to prevent their recurrence [16].

- Problem solving: To analyze the causes of a specific problem and find effective solutions [17].

- Decision making: To evaluate different options and make informed decisions [18].

- Planning: To identify factors that may affect the success of a project and develop action plans to mitigate risks [19].

In the case study, the main question is: What are the reasons that explain the lack of integration of IoT in the Spanish university educational environment as a tool to support teaching?

Through a panel of experts developed by Ishikawa's matrix, a diverse panel of experts covering a variety of relevant knowledge areas is needed to fully understand the causes of the lack of integration of AI in the Spanish university educational environment. The expert panel was composed of: artificial intelligence experts, university professors, educational administrators, education researchers, representatives of technology companies, as well as university students.

4. Challenges faced by the integration of IoT in Spanish universities: results and analysis

Once the process of analyzing results and conclusions was completed, an exhaustive compilation and analysis of the data obtained in each round of the Delphi panel were carried out, allowing patterns to be identified and a consensus to be reached among the experts.

The categories obtained with their subcategories are (**Figure 2**).

C1. People, training, and knowledge about IoT:

- C1.1. Unrealistic expectations about IoT capabilities.
- C1.2. Disinterest or lack of motivation among the teaching staff.
- C1.3.Negative perception of IoT by students.
- C1.4 Lack of digital skills in students.

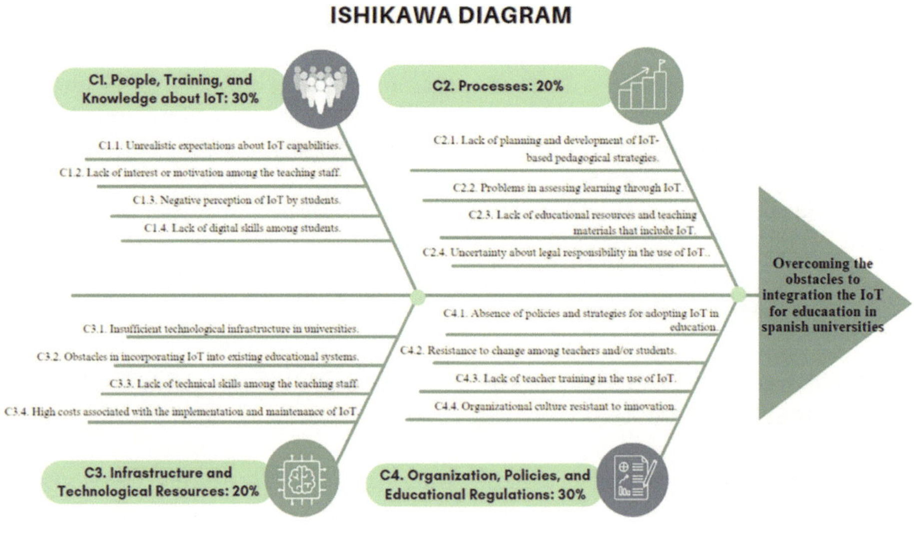

Figure 2.
Ishikawa diagram. Source: own elaboration.

This factor is crucial, as without the necessary knowledge and skills, IoT implementation will be difficult. However, lack of training alone is not the only obstacle.

C1 WEIGHT. 30%.

C2. Processes:

- C2.1. Lack of planning and development of IoT-based pedagogical strategies.
- C2.2. Problems in the assessment of learning using IoT.
- C2.3. Lack of educational resources and teaching materials that include IoT.
- C2.4. Uncertainty about legal liability in the use of IoT.

This factor can be just as important as training, as resistance to change can be a major obstacle to the adoption of new technologies.

C2 WEIGHT. 20%.

C3. Infrastructure and technological resources:

- C3.1 Insufficiency of technological infrastructure in universities.
- C3.2. Obstacles in the incorporation of IoT into existing education systems.
- C3.3. Lack of technical skills on the part of the teaching staff.
- C3.4. High costs associated with the implementation and maintenance of IoT.

It's an important factor, but its impact can vary by college. Some universities already have the basic infrastructure in place, while others need to invest more in this aspect.

C3 WEIGHT. 20%.

C4. Educational organization, policies, and regulations:

- C4.1. Absence of policies and strategies for the adoption of IoT in education.
- C4.2. Resistance to change among teachers and/or students.
- C4.3. Lack of teacher training in the use of IoT.
- C4.4. Organizational culture is resistant to innovation.

This factor can be a significant obstacle, especially if policies and regulations are not up-to-date to adapt to new technologies such as AI.

C4 WEIGHT. 30%.

This analysis examines in depth the challenges faced by Spanish university education in the adoption of IoT to support teaching, focusing on four main categories:

- C1. People, training, and IoT knowledge
- C2. Processes

- C3. Infrastructure and rechnological resources
- C4. Educational organization, policies, and regulations

The category "C1. People, Training, and Knowledge about IoT" addresses various aspects related to the acceptance and integration of IoT in the university educational environment. Among the causes identified are disinterest or lack of motivation on the part of teachers, which may be influenced by a lack of familiarity with technology, the perception of IoT as a threat to their work, or resistance to change. In addition, students' negative perception of IoT, their limited digital skills, and unrealistic expectations about IoT capabilities also contribute to this lack of integration. To address these challenges, it is recommended to develop awareness-raising and training programs for faculty, foster a culture of digital learning among students, and establish an open dialog on the ethical and educational implications of IoT in university education. These measures could help overcome barriers and promote more effective integration of IoT into the educational environment.

The category "C2. Processes" addresses crucial aspects related to the successful integration of artificial intelligence (AI) in the university educational environment. Challenges are identified in key areas, such as pedagogical planning, learning assessment, availability of educational resources, and legal accountability. Failure to plan and design pedagogical strategies with IoT can result in inconsistent implementation and underutilization of their capabilities for learning personalization. IoT learning assessment presents challenges in data selection and analysis, which can impact the accurate determination of data impact and fairness in assessment. The scarcity of IoT educational resources and uncertainty about legal liabilities also pose significant obstacles. To address these challenges, it is recommended to foster multidisciplinary collaboration, develop effective pedagogical strategies, design specific assessment tools, and establish clear policies on the ethical use of IoT in university education. These measures can facilitate a more effective and responsible integration of IoT in education.

The category "C3. Infrastructure and Technological Resources" in Ishikawa's matrix addresses the technical and infrastructural challenges that hinder the effective integration of IoT in Spanish university education. The four main obstacles identified are as follows: the lack of adequate technological infrastructure in universities, difficulties in the integration of IoT with existing educational systems, lack of technical knowledge on the part of teachers, and high costs of implementation and maintenance of IoT. To overcome these challenges, recommendations are proposed, such as investing in the modernization of technological infrastructure, promoting collaboration and interoperability, offering IoT training for teachers, and exploring alternative funding models and public-private collaborations. These actions can contribute to facilitating the adoption and effective use of IoT in Spanish university education, thus promoting innovation and educational advancement in the country.

The category "C4. Educational Organization, Policies, and Regulations" in Ishikawa's matrix explores the challenges related to the effective implementation of IoT in the Spanish university educational environment. Four main obstacles are identified: the lack of defined policies and strategies, resistance to change by teachers and/or students, lack of teacher training in the use of IoT, and an organizational culture resistant to innovation. To address these challenges, recommendations are proposed, such as developing clear policies and strategies, implementing awareness and communication programs to address resistance to change, and providing IoT training opportunities for faculty. These actions can help overcome organizational barriers and promote more effective integration of IoT into university education, thus fostering innovation and educational progress in the country.

5. Ishikawa diagram conclusions

In conclusion, the effective adoption of IoT in Spanish university education to support teaching faces a number of significant challenges ranging from lack of planning and leadership to resistance to change and lack of preparation of both faculty and students. These challenges require a comprehensive approach involving all relevant actors, including political and university leadership, faculty, students, businesses, and organizations. It is essential to invest in technological infrastructure, provide adequate training, create appropriate teaching materials, and foster a culture of innovation to fully realize the potential of IoT in education.

The adoption of IoT in Spanish university education is expected to have a positive impact on the quality of learning, accessibility, efficiency, and innovation. To advance in this process, it is recommended to establish a multidisciplinary working group, increase investment in research and innovation, promote collaboration between different entities, and raise awareness among the educational community about the benefits of IoT for education. Ultimately, addressing these challenges requires a continuous and collaborative commitment from all stakeholders to create a brighter and more equitable future for learning in Spanish university education.

En las decisiones estratégicas de la adopción de la tecnología además de aspectos funcionales cada vez más se tienen en cuenta otros aspectos importantes como temas de accesibilidad o protección de datos personales.

The pandemic has acted as a catalyst for the adoption of educational technologies at all levels of education. The report presented corroborates this, evidencing a significant increase in the interest, use, and incorporation of these tools in the university environment.

We are in the process of configuring a new educational scenario, where some changes driven by the pandemic have been consolidated, while others are in the process of adapting or have even regressed toward the pre-pandemic model.

It is crucial to take an in-depth look at these changes and their long-term implications. There is a need to identify successful practices that have emerged during the crisis and assess their sustainability in the future. Likewise, it is essential to understand the challenges that still persist and work together to overcome them.

Here are some key points to consider in this new educational landscape:

- Need for a critical evaluation of educational technologies: It is important to assess the effectiveness and real impact of technological tools on learning, considering not only their potential but also their limitations and possible negative effects.

- Promoting equity and inclusion: The integration of educational technologies must be done in an equitable manner, ensuring that all students have access to the necessary tools and resources, regardless of their socioeconomic background or geographic location.

- Strengthening teacher education: It is critical to provide teachers with the necessary training and support to effectively integrate educational technologies into their pedagogical practices.
- Redefinition of the role of the teacher: In this new scenario, the role of the teacher is not limited to transmitting knowledge, but becomes a guide, facilitator, and mentor who accompanies students in their learning process.
- Fostering collaboration and teamwork: Educational technologies can be valuable tools to promote collaboration among students, teachers, and even educational institutions.
- Adaptation to learning needs and styles: Technological tools must be flexible and adapt to the different needs and learning styles of students.
- Data protection and privacy: It is essential to ensure the protection of personal data and the privacy of students in the digital educational environment.

6. Future strategies and recommendations

The integration of IoT in the university has enormous potential to transform learning, research, and institutional management. By combining an innovative culture, strong digital literacy, robust pedagogical strategies, and modern infrastructure, universities can create an ecosystem that drives effective IoT use and prepares students for the future of work.

The successful integration of IoT in Spanish universities requires a comprehensive and strategic approach. Based on our analysis, we propose the following strategies and recommendations:

Fostering a culture of innovation: the integration of the Internet of Things (IoT) in the university requires an environment that encourages experimentation and creativity. To this end, spaces for collaboration must be created, policies to support innovation must be implemented and a culture of continuous learning must be promoted. In addition, it is important to recognize and reward successful initiatives and projects related to the IoT.

Development of robust IoT-based pedagogical strategies: The integration of IoT in education must go beyond the simple acquisition of technical knowledge. It is necessary to incorporate IoT-related content into the curriculum of various disciplines and to encourage collaborative projects between students, professors, and industrial partners.

Investment in modern infrastructure: To take full advantage of IoT technologies, it is necessary to have a modern infrastructure that includes high-speed Internet, smart classrooms, and IoT devices. In addition, pilot programs should be implemented to test the feasibility and effectiveness of IoT solutions before wider deployment.

Improving digital literacy: It is essential to improve the digital skills and familiarity with IoT technologies of the university community. To achieve this, continuing education programs must be developed that include introductory courses, specialized courses, and practical workshops. In addition, workshops and seminars should be organized to showcase the practical applications of IoT in educational settings and foster connections with industry.

7. Step-by-step framework for implementation

To offer practical guidance to university administrators and policymakers, we propose the following step-by-step framework for the implementation of IoT solutions (**Figure 3**).

1. Evaluation and planning:

    - Assess needs: Identify objectives, analyze the environment and user needs.

    - Strategic planning: Establish priorities and goals, allocate resources, define a schedule, and communicate a plan.

2. Infrastructure development:

    - Technology upgrade: Hardware, software, network, and security improvements.

    - Pilot testing: Evaluate effectiveness in real-world educational settings, identify challenges, collect data, and refine solutions.

3. Capacity development:

    - Training programs: Train teachers, administrative staff, and students.

    - Student engagement: Clubs, workshops, contests, research, and entrepreneurship opportunities.

4. Implementation and monitoring:

    - Deployment: Implement IoT solutions across the university.

    - Continuous monitoring: Establish a monitoring and evaluation system to ensure effectiveness and sustainability.

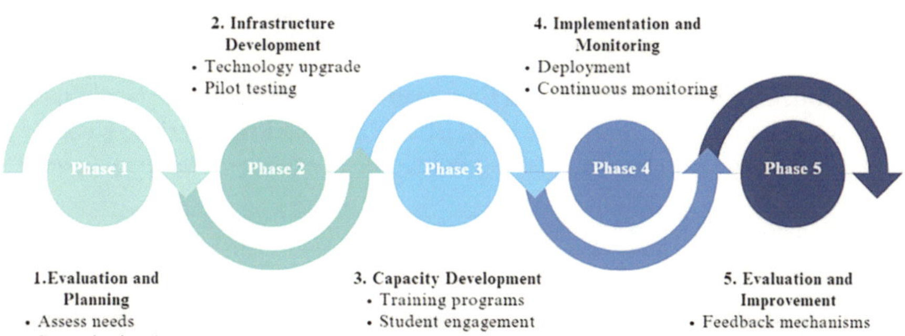

Figure 3.
Framework for implementation. Source: own elaboration.

5. Evaluation and improvement:

    - Feedback mechanisms: Collect information from all stakeholders.

    - Continuous improvement: Using feedback to make improvements to IoT initiatives and address emerging challenges.

In conclusion, harnessing the Internet of Things (IoT) to its full potential within Spanish universities necessitates a multi-pronged approach that tackles technological hurdles, educational gaps, and policy restrictions. By prioritizing initiatives that cultivate digital literacy among students and faculty, bolster technological infrastructure, and encourage collaborative innovation across departments, universities can unlock the transformative potential of IoT. This strategic approach has the power to revolutionize higher education in Spain, ushering in a new era of enriched learning experiences and groundbreaking research opportunities.

Conflict of interest

The authors declare no conflict of interest.

Author details

Nicoletta González-Cancelas*, Alberto Camarero-Orive and Javier Vaca-Cabrero
Department of Transport, Territorial and Urban Planning Engineering, ETSI Caminos, Canales y Puertos, Universidad Politécnica de Madrid, Madrid, Spain

*Address all correspondence to: nicoleta.gcancelas@upm.es

References

[1] Li K et al. When internet of things meets metaverse: Convergence of physical and cyber worlds. IEEE Internet of Things Journal. 2022;**10**(5):4148-4173

[2] Miñano Rubio R, Uribe D, Moreno-Romero A, Yáñez S. Embedding sustainability competences into engineering education. The case of informatics engineering and industrial engineering degree programs at Spanish universities. Sustainability. 2019;**11**(20):5832

[3] Pal D, Zhang X, Siyal S. Prohibitive factors to the acceptance of internet of things (IoT) technology in society: A smart-home context using a resistive modelling approach. Technology in Society. 2021;**66**:101683

[4] Rodríguez-Abitia G, Martínez-Pérez S, Ramirez-Montoya MS, Lopez-Caudana E. Digital gap in universities and challenges for quality education: A diagnostic study in Mexico and Spain. Sustainability. 2020;**12**(21):9069

[5] Sánchez-Barrioluengo M. Articulating the "three-missions" in Spanish universities. Research Policy. 2014;**43**(10):1760-1773

[6] Prendes-Espinosa MP, Gutiérrez-Porlán I, García-Tudela PA. Collaborative work in higher education: Tools and strategies to implement the e-assessment. In: Workgroups e-Assessment: Planning, Implementing and Analysing Frameworks. Singapore: Springer; 2021. pp. 55-84

[7] Perera VH, Moriña A, Sánchez-Díaz N, Spinola-Elias Y. Technological platforms for inclusive practice at university: A qualitative analysis from the perspective of Spanish faculty members. Sustainability. 2021;**13**(9):4755

[8] Fuentes Pardo JM, Ramírez Gómez Á, García García AI, Ayuga Téllez F. Web-based education in Spanish universities. A comparison of open source E-learning platforms. Journal of Systemics, Cybernetics and Informatics. 2012;**10**(6):47-53

[9] Ramírez-Montoya MS, Loaiza-Aguirre MI, Zúñiga-Ojeda A, Portuguez-Castro M. Characterization of the teaching profile within the framework of education 4.0. Future Internet. 2021;**13**(4):91

[10] Alannasir W. Characteristic-based development students aspect. International Journal of Asian Education. 2020;**1**(1):29-36

[11] Weil C, Bibri SE, Longchamp R, Golay F, Alahi A. Urban digital twin challenges: A systematic review and perspectives for sustainable smart cities. Sustainable Cities and Society. 2023;**99**:104862

[12] Liesa-Orús M, Latorre-Cosculluela C, Vázquez-Toledo S, Sierra-Sánchez V. The technological challenge facing higher education professors: Perceptions of ICT tools for developing 21st century skills. Sustainability. 2020;**12**(13):5339

[13] Cheung SK, Kwok LF, Phusavat K, Yang HH. Shaping the future learning environments with smart elements: Challenges and opportunities. International Journal of Educational Technology in Higher Education. 2021;**18**:1-9

[14] Fitria TN. Doing manual paraphrasing: What should the students do in paraphrasing or rewriting English writing? SALEE: Study of Applied Linguistics and English Education. 2024;**5**(1):25-43

[15] González-Cancelas N, Cabrero JV, Orive AC, Párraga MJM, Gutierrez DD, Santiago JIP. Assessing port sustainability in ecuador using an Ishikawa diagram. World Scientific News. 2023;**186**:12-26

[16] Liliana L. A new model of Ishikawa diagram for quality assessment. In: Iop Conference Series: Materials Science and Engineering. IOP Publishing; 2016. p. 012099. Available from: https://www.researchgate.net/publication/311341507_A_new_model_of_Ishikawa_diagram_for_quality_assessment

[17] Pavlovic D, Todorovic M, Mladenovic S, Milosavljevic P. The role of quality methods in improving education process: Case study. Serbian Journal of Management. 2014;**9**(2):219-230

[18] Elsayed K, Daif R. Use of the Ishikawa diagram to understand the employees' perceptions towards nepotism in tourism and hospitality industry. Journal of Tourism and Hospitality Management. 2019;**7**(2)

[19] Rodgers M, Oppenheim R. Ishikawa diagrams and Bayesian belief networks for continuous improvement applications. The TQM Journal. 2019;**31**(3):294-318. DOI: 10.1108/TQM-11-2018-0184

Chapter 5

Perspective Chapter: The Evolution of Edge Computing in the IoT Era of the Twenty-Second Century

Faith Nwokoma and Cajetan M. Akujuobi

Abstract

Motivated by global technological advancements, this paper explores the relationship between edge computing and the Internet of Things (IoT) as society approaches the twenty-second century. Utilizing both case studies and impact assessment approaches, the paper emphasizes the evolution of these technologies, their application areas, and their societal implications. Cloud computing has traditionally dominated large-scale data processing and storage, while IoT and edge computing enable ubiquitous computing with a focus on endpoint sensing and near-field computation, respectively. Technological leaps facilitated by edge computing include advancements in sensory applications, artificial intelligence, and nanotechnology, promising transformative impacts across sectors. Examples include automated metering and real-time analytics in homes, as well as improved healthcare through efficient video surveillance, energy management, environmental monitoring, and logistics. Edge computing's societal impacts span smart city development, enhanced healthcare services, environmental sustainability, and economic growth through innovative business models and job creation. This paper establishes a foundation for the efficient integration of edge computing in IoT discussions as society prepares for the challenges and opportunities of the twenty-second century.

Keywords: edge computing, internet of things, century, evolution, smart devices, smart city

1. Introduction

The dawn of the twenty-first century has seen a vast change in technology and Internet of Things (IoT) has significantly benefited and changed our everyday life. That digital transformation is known as "Internet of Things" (IoT) and it is changed from future concept to our needed item for daily lives [1]. This transformation is widely acknowledged and in nearly every industry from healthcare to agriculture to urban planning to transportation, smart devices have brought forth the kind of automation, efficiency, and connectedness that would have been impossible to imagine just half a century ago. With each advancement, there come new opportunities and obstacles which demand a deeper grasp of what they entail. Internet of Things (IoT) is typically a global network system that has physical objects with the embedded sensors and the actuator, and the data collected through these objects are passed over a network without requiring human-to-human or human-to-computer interaction [2, 3]. They communicate via networks that are familiar (Wi-Fi, Bluetooth, NFC, RFID and Zigbee) as well as different, like GSM, GPRS, 3G and LTE for a wide-area options. Gathering, aggregating, processing and some storage may be taken part at the local system to made full utilization of its functionalities along with connectivities [3]. The technology provides answers that do anything from saving energy, making us more secure, keeping us healthy or educated, performing better at work and helping us make better decisions in factories, retail stores or farms (**Figure 1**).

The concept of a network of smart devices was discussed as early as 1982, with a modified Coke machine at Carnegie Mellon University becoming the first Internet-connected appliance, able to report its inventory and whether newly loaded drinks were cold [5, 6]. The field of the IoT as we now know it is estimated around 1999, by Kevin Ashton of MIT's Auto-ID Center. Since then, the spectrum covered by the IoT has been expanded with non-electronic items and everyday objects, such as food or household items, being connected to the internet as well. The ideas encapsulated here are far-reaching in that they are instrumental in painting the picture of what the Internet of Things is supposed to accomplish: converting mundane items into connected devices that work in tandem to speak to each other to streamline facets of life and industry.

The amount of data from IoTs and mobile devices for instance, wearables and sensors requires it to be processed in a way that exposes their constrained energy and processing power. These constraints are usually avoided by handling computation and storage by the elastic, demand-based cloud. But cloud data centers are far from the consumers and thus communication latency is high and link usage is stressed. A further challenge of centralized cloud computing and IoT-based systems is resolved by edge computing, which is a distributed model that processes and stores data at the network edge level [5]. It minimizes communication latency, optimizes the speed at which computations are carried out, and enables unprecedented real-time analysis and decision making when compute resources are placed closer to where data is being created (**Figure 2**).

To overcome such barriers, Edge Computing positions systems close to the creation points of the data [6]. More specifically, to avoid the creation of large centralized data centres this architecture distributes computing assets across many other devices. EC also provides the advantage of performing analysis and reaction in real time because data processed are localized, something that is vital in applications that need to produce quick responses [7]. Because it decentralizes server operations,

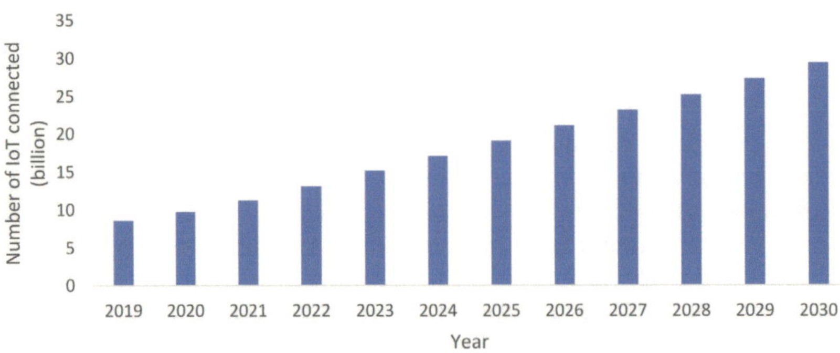

Figure 1.
Number of IoT devices worldwide. Source: Kumar et al. [4].

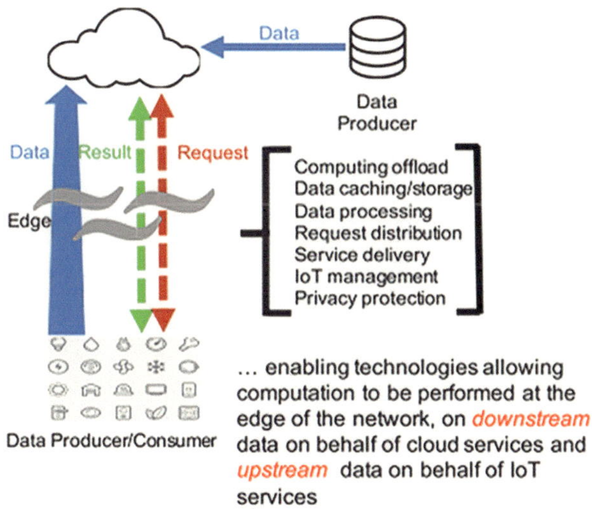

Figure 2.
Simplified view of edge computing. Source: Abdul-Qawy et al. [2].

it shrinks bandwidth consumption, progresses in efficiency, and grows to include more edge devices while doing so, without a glitch [8]. Edge computing is based on distributing data processing and storage to the edge devices which are in proximity to the origin of data contrary to traditional cloud computing where data centers are centralized. As a result of limiting send / receive data transfer to a central server this also minimizes latency and reaction time and optimizes bandwidth. This makes system dependability improve by dispersing resources and reducing the risk of having single points of failure and also enhances protection of sensitive data locally thereby enhancing the privacy and security of data that is being stored [9]. For edge computing and IoT, ECDriven-IoT systems enhance nearfield computing and vicinity perception due to the distinctness of their approaches.

In light of the above, the main objective of this study is to explore the relationship between edge computing and the Internet of Things (IoT) as society approaches the twenty-second century.

From the discussions, the hypothesis that can be drawn from this study is stated as:

H_0: edge computing has a significant relationship with Internet of Things (IoT) in the twenty-second century.

H_1: edge computing has a significant relationship with Internet of Things (IoT) in the twenty-second century.

2. Literature review

2.1 IoT-edge computing nexus

See **Figure 3**.

With an emphasis on localized data processing and analysis, Edge Computing's integration with the Internet of Things (IoT) heralds in a new era in computer architecture. In order to support real-time data processing and decision-making, this approach

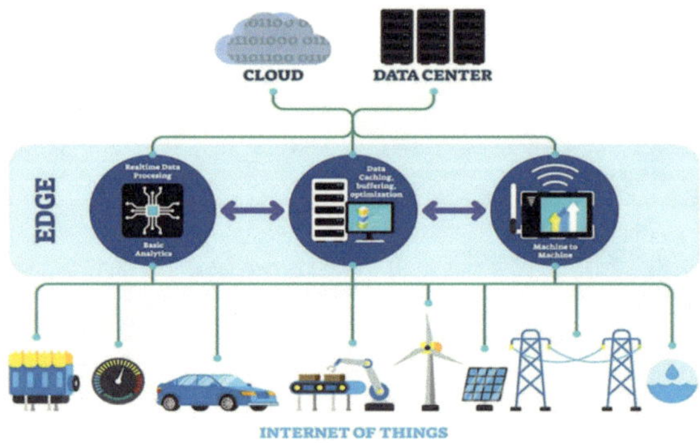

Figure 3.
Relationship between IoT and Edge Computing. Source: Sodiya et al. [10].

entails strategically placing computing resources at the edge of the network [11]. IoT devices act as data endpoints, gathering and sending data to adjacent edge devices or nodes that are capable of processing computations. Real-time data processing, filtering, and analysis by these edge devices allows for autonomous decision-making based on pre-established guidelines or machine learning algorithms. Following processing, data can be sent to cloud servers that are centrally located for additional analysis, archiving, or system integration [12].

Being an extension of Big Data concepts with an incorporation of distributed data analysis, Edge Computing together with IoT paves the way for a new generation of computer architecture. To generate such possibilities, this has the tendency of placing computing resources closer to the real-time/data-processing-decision-making parts of the network [11]. IoT devices serve as data sources and sinks that collect data and transmit it to other close-by edge devices or nodes that are equipped for completing calculations. The capability of Processing, filtering and analysis in these edge devices for real-time allows decision making with reference to defined guidelines or ML models. Data can then be forwarded to cloud servers that are centrally structured for further processing, analysis, or storage or as part of a larger system [12].

Concerning IoT, edge computing highlights on the closeness, scalability, and decentralization to enhance LLA, EEP, and DM for IT fitness [13]. Two key benefits: lower latency which equates to better response time, this is crucial in applications such as real-time surveillance, autopilot vehicles, and fabrication. The central idea of using edge computing is to minimize the data traffic while optimizing the storage space for data processing. In that, it enhances data security and privacy through reducing transmission risks by ensuring data is retained closer to source [10]. These are the innovative, flexible and future-proof solutions that are provided by edge computing to address varying workloads. It ensures that the IoT devices operate autonomously by allowing them to run parallel to a network, thus ensuring that it will continue to work even if the latter has experienced a system failure. This integration has kept on encouraging innovations in industries leading to improvement on productivity and provision of opportunities that may have not been considered earlier [10]. Edge computing aids in quality control, predictive repair, and real-time scrutinizing means in the industrial business [13]. They enhance patient care and organizational effectiveness in the numerous industries involved with healthcare through support of telehealth and distant patient management [10, 13, 14]. Edge computing helps with environmental monitoring, public safety, and traffic control in smart city programs. It improves supply chain optimization, inventory management, and personalized shopping in the retail industry [15].

2.2 The synergy between IoT and edge computing: the evolution of IoT

The evolution of IoT has gone through many stages. These stages have been outlined from the beginning of Nikol Tesla's innovation to its current state the world is enjoying of aspects of the IoT.

2.2.1 Nikola Tesla's inventions

Radio communication and the delivery of alternating current electrical ability fashionable in the present day were improved by the ingenious Serbian born American inventor Nikola Tesla. He filed an application in 1891 that led to the granting of a patent on the Tesla coil, a high-voltage and high-frequency transformer applied in radio technology [16]. Later that year he also showed wireless transmission using the 'Tesla coil' he also learned that he could transmit and receive radio waves only if the frequency matched. Around 1893, Tesla had developed and successfully demonstrated what could be considered the rudimentary wireless telecommunication implementing a radio transmitter and a radio receiver [16]. His experiments in 1897 continued to show him achieving successful long range radio communication.

2.2.2 RFID

RFID technology is basically based on radio-frequency identification of objects through the transmission of radio waves [17]. To make the process global and real-time, you simply connect an RFID reader to a network, which is the Internet. Modern RFID is commonly thought to have originated in and after the Second World War radar developments and Harry Stockman, 1948 paper on point-to-point using radio signals. The first notable usage involved the IFF system which stands for identification, friend or foe during the Second World War. Other early milestones included Sensormatic and Checkpoint emerging in the1960s to invent anti-shoplifting systems [17]. The 1970s were the most productive in terms of academic development, particularly, Mario W. Cardulla applied for the invention of active RFID tags which was later joined by Charles Walton who applies for passive RFID tag invention. It has been increasingly used in transportation sector, logistics industry and manufacturing industries by 1980s.

2.2.3 The ARPANET

E-networks started with the development of Advanced Research Projects Agency Network (ARPANET) which was established by United States Department of Defense's ARPA in 1966 [18]. The first computers connected are called ARPAnet in 1969, between UCLA and Stanford Research Institute. Originally operational in 1975, ARPANET grew throughout the 1980s and was terminated in 1990 to create for the use of the more public Internet. To recall, the company launched the first connected soda machine late last year in New York City exclusively for the company's employees. Back in 1982, a team of students from Carnegie Mellon University invented what can be termed as the first internet, or rather World Wide Web enabled soda dispensing machine. This was achieving its goals because it used ARPANET to monitor the state of the machine so that the users did not have to manually check if it was empty.

2.2.4 The creation of the TCP/I invoked protocol

TCP/IP protocol which has been selected as one of the standards for ARPANET in 1983 has become the Internet's essence. Described by Robert E. Kahn and Vinton Cerf, it established the basic principles of data packetization, emission, and reception to achieve a strong and adaptive form of data transmission.

2.2.5 Autonomous navigation

NavLab was built by Carnegie Mellon University in 1984 as an experimental platform for autonomous vehicles. Organized under grants from DARPA, driving a project that resulted to development of NavLab 1 in 1986, it became the pioneer in the area of autonomous navigation.

2.2.6 Growth of the internet: the world wide web

The world wide web by Tim Berners-Lee: In 1989 he imagined the WWW which in 1991 began to be lived. He initialized World Wide Web Consortium W3C in 1994 that targets to establish web standards for the global community. Many mainstream internet users emerged in mid 1990s to enhance the communication and commercial applications of the WWW.

2.2.7 Early IoT devices

The Internet of Things or IoT started in or around 1990 when John Romkey created a remote-control toaster [19]. Late 90s to early years of the twenty-first century saw other evolutionary inventions such as the celebrated 1993 Trojan Room Coffee Pot webcam and Nabaztag, a teddy bear like early home automation system, built in 2005. The IoT period emerged by the year 2008 and ever since; internet connected devices exceeded the total global population.

2.2.8 Introduction of wearables

Wearable technology though came to light with Steve Mann backpacked computer in the year 1981 and the first smart watch in the year 1998. Introductions of 'Internet of Medical Things or (IoMT),' who monitor heartbeat or glucose levels, came to healthcare, forecasted to be worth $176 billion by 2026 [19]. The term was first used by Kevin Ashton in 1998 to describe the famous RFID system used in tracking supply chain product inventory. Kevin Ashton first used the term Internet of Things in 1999 in an elevator pitch portraying a retail tracking initiative to Procter & Gamble. The term came into mainstream use in 2004 and was further popularized in 2014 when Google bought Nest and it made an appearance at CES.

2.2.9 Internet-enabled appliances

When Bluetooth 1 appeared in the market it introduced so many things. Early estimates of TV-PC convergence to 0 in 1999 paved way to internet. Aparatus like LG's

2000 Internet Digital DIOS refrigerator. Despite initial high prices, the market for connected appliances grew, with increasing demand for IoT devices.

2.2.10 IoT is born

The concept of IoT was first discussed around 2008. Nest of the Google group created smart home appliances by the year 2010 [19]. Cisco systems predicted that the start of the IoT or Internet of Things began between the years 2008 to 2009 where more devices were connected than the world's population.

2.2.11 LPWAN

Low-Power Wide-Area Network (LPWAN) is a type of IoT link that allows low-data-rate and long-range communication. LPWANs were invented in the late 1980s, while some of the most advanced technologies such as Sigfox, LoRaWAN, LTE-M, and NB-IoT came to existence in the 2000s to allow for real time monitoring and integration of remote devices. Satellite IoT has been defined as the next step in IoT evolution that has not been fully developed.

2.2.12 Emergency of IoT

Satellite IoT, also employed in telemetry since the 1970s, has recently draw more attention given the cost reduction and novel technologies. Satellite IoT is used for monitoring and tracking in hard to reach places while hybrid approach allows for switching between cellular and satellite links seamlessly.

2.3 Evolution of edge computing

Edge computing was first introduced in the early 19090's when Akamai technology delivered CDN which enabled encoded content like pictures and videos to

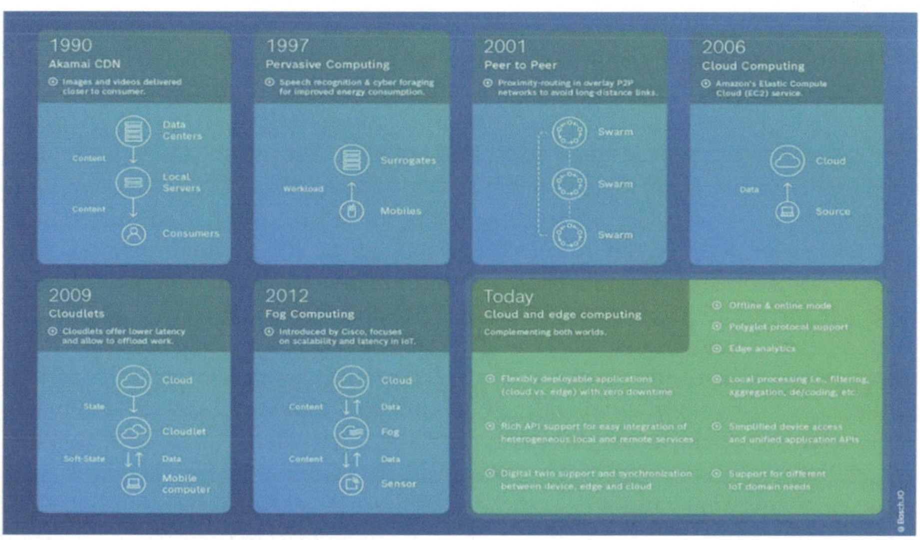

Figure 4.
Evolution of edge computing. Source: De Donno et al. [20].

be processed at the nodes that are closer to the users [10, 14]. In 1997, Nobel et al. provided a proof of concept of using servers to perform tasks that would otherwise be performed by the handicap small appliances in agile application-aware adaptation for mobility (**Figure 4**) [13].

This concept is now evident in services such as Google, Apple, and Amazon's speech recognition. Ref. [13] built on this with their 2001 paper on pervasive computing, proposing decentralized applications over P2P networks for scaling and redundant routing and load balancing of the network load and latency. Cloud computing, specifically Amazon's Elastic Compute Cloud introduced in 2006, greatly impacted edge computing through resourceful computing visualization and storage. But this was not suitable for all cases where there is a need for immediate local computing as we have seen in self-driving cars and industrial IoT. Ref. [13] suggested the idea of cloudlet and the adoption of a two-tier architecture where cloudlets offer lower latency to nearby mobile gadgets. That is why, in 2012, Cisco introduced the concept of "fog computing" to address IoT issues and support large numbers of devices and data with real-time, low-latency applications [6, 10]. Today, cloud computing is universal storage and computation, and edge computing quickly processes data locally, relaying less to the backend and handling sensitive data.

3. Methodology

The methodology of the case study and impact assessment were both used in the work to treat in detail the passages of real-world uses and societal ramification passages of edge computing on the Internet of Things [19, 21]. Case studies on concrete examples of edge computing and Internet of Things applications in industries such as automated home analytics and metering, better healthcare through effective video surveillance, energy management, environment and logistics monitoring, were reviewed. The review of these instances showed the practical applications for these technologies and their advantages. This approach also provided an in-depth understanding of technological challenges and successes encountered in various situations [19]. For example, studies on edge computing implementation in smart city projects would provide information on how these technologies make urban life better by providing infrastructure and services such as real-time analytics and automated metering in homes, enhanced health through effective energy management, video surveillance, environmental monitoring, and logistics. The impact assessment was necessary in order to analyze the broader social implications of the confluence of edge computing and IoT [21]. This involved assessing the effects on smart city development, healthcare delivery, environmental sustainability, and economic growth. The societal effects were reviewed through responses to how these technologies improve people's quality of life, economic innovation with employment growth, and environmental sustainability. For instance, the efficiency of edge computing in improving environmental policies and practices is applied to improve smart city development, healthcare services, environmental sustainability, and economic growth. When getting ready for all chances and challenges this century will bring, this integrated methodology shall ensure that the paper not only talks about the technological advancement and applications of Edge Computing and IoT but also about their significant societal implications. Finally, data acquired were analysis based on various themes in relation to the areas of life that have been affected by edge computing as well as the societal impact of edge on societal existence.

4. Results and discussion

4.1 Interplay of IoT and edge computing: applications, benefits and challenges

4.1.1 Applications

In line with [21, 22], there are a variety of ways that IoT and Edge Computing interplay which includes:

- *Smart homes and cities:* With these IoT devices, the smart homes application domain of edge computing is evolving. These devices help in performing and metering utilities such as water, electricity, and gas through real-time analytics processed on the edge. It also applies to the smart cities where it improves control of the streetlights, quality of air and water, paths in the case of disasters and watering of the gardens.

- *Healthcare:* Edge computing has transformed the healthcare system through constant and timely interaction with health data of different devices [19]. First of all, while adjusting IoT for healthcare one come across a certain problem of latency for cloud computing; however, edge computing solves the mentioned issues, thus enhancing the effectiveness and speed of IoT healthcare applications.

- *Edge computing in video surveillance:* Edge sensors deployed for smart video surveillance in domestic security and anti-terrorism enable real-time processing of multiple cameras and sensor video data for processing storage of video data. This system efficiently plans and extracts the essential information to cope with security researchers.

- *Smart grid:* Real-time sensing and processing of consumption and distribution patterns will be possible in smart energy management through edge computing. It cooperates with cloud computing to process big data in flexible and reliable power grid designs.

Environmental Monitoring: Edge and cloud computing make environmental monitoring systems more efficient. In agriculture, forestry, food safety, for example, the automation of applications on the Internet follow important parameters such as gas concentrations, water levels, lighting, soil humidity, land changes etc.

4.1.2 Benefits

ECDriven-IoT has several benefits for IoT Applications. The first one is about the geographical location - since edge servers are closer to IoT devices than the cloud, it guarantees real-time response with low network latency, helping provide higher Quality of Service (QoS). Due to the proximity of the MEC to the user equipment, it performs SLA to high request real-time IoT applications, resulting in a better service quality to the application and lesser amount of off load data to cloud [11]. It also reduces the consumption of energy. The common situation where IoT nodes, inherently with very limited power sources, consume a large amount of power to synchronize large volumes of data to remote and distant clouds. Edge computing sends the data to nearby edge servers and, in turn, reduces the usage of energy used by the IoT nodes, increasing their life and lowering maintenance costs [21]. Third, ECDriven-IoT is highly scalable It's not uncommon for a cloud-based Internet of Things system to come up against what a large-scale access issues, with hordes of simultaneous connections attempting to be maintained - and a standard login-queue not being an option. ECDriven-IoT relies on a number of low compute, distributed edge servers to provide limited compute resources, to enable scalability for big-data IoT applications such as driverless cars and smart cities [11]. So edge computing is popular in many academic institutions such as Internet of Things thereafter.

4.1.3 Challenges

In Internet of Things-based edge computing, heterogeneity refers to the diversity of computer and Communication technologies in the context of Internet of Things-based edge computing [1, 23]. Even though the characteristics of communication technologies especially data rate, transmission range, and bandwidth, are different in each other, the properties of computing platforms such as different hardware design and OS, are also varied. As edge devices host varying applications, developing portable software solutions across such environments is necessary. However, present software ideas remain hardware-specific, and do not much more than cover heterogeneous issues entirely. In this context, where various IoT devices and sensors communicate with edge servers and one another via distinct communication protocols, standard protocols and interfaces are crucial. There are many different device vendors, and technology is advancing quickly, so creating these standards is difficult.

Standards are very important in such context as the communication among diverse communication protocols in which implement IoT devices and sensors as well as the edge servers themselves. There are thousands of device vendors and technology is moving fast, so it is challenging to create these standards. At the heart of IoT-based edge computing, availability focuses on mean time between failures, failure probability, and mean time to recovery, and ensures that these variables are in place for ongoing hardware and software resource availability at the endpoint for subscription devices. Availability optimization [5, 6, 12] focuses on minimizing downtime incidents and maximizing operational uptime.

There are additional difficulties with data abstraction and security. Large volumes of raw data are produced by IoT devices, and preprocessing at the gateway level is necessary for functions like event detection, privacy protection, and noise reduction. It is still difficult to strike a balance between privacy concerns and data utility, which makes it necessary to carefully control data visibility to apps on edge devices in order to successfully reduce security threats.

4.2 Innovations at the edge: shaping the future of IoT

4.2.1 Technological advances

Future advancements in the Internet of Things (IoT) and edge computing are set to revolutionize numerous industries with innovations in sensors, artificial intelligence (AI), and nanotechnology [6]. Emerging sensor technologies, especially those leveraging nanotechnology, promise smaller, more precise sensors that can be embedded in diverse environments. This development enhances data accuracy in fields like healthcare, agriculture, and environmental monitoring, facilitating real-time decision-making as highlighted in MIT Technology Review and IoT For All. Integrating edge AI with smart sensors enables local data processing, reducing latency crucial for applications such as autonomous vehicles and smart cities [11].

Advances in AI include edge AI and TinyML, allowing AI algorithms to operate directly on edge devices like sensors and gateways [24]. This capability supports real-time processing without relying on centralized cloud servers, essential for sectors like industrial automation and healthcare monitoring as discussed in IoT For All. TinyML enables lightweight machine learning models on small, resource-constrained devices, broadening applications in wearables and smart home devices [9]. Innovations in edge computing include federated learning, enhancing privacy by training machine learning models on local data without sharing it, pivotal for sensitive sectors such as finance and healthcare [10, 19]. Specialized edge computing hardware like AI accelerators and modular chiplets, described in MIT Technology Review, promise enhanced processing power and efficiency, further bolstering IoT capabilities across industries. Additionally, advancements in nanotechnology, including nanomaterials and nano-robots, are poised to improve durability, efficiency, and scalability of IoT devices in areas like renewable energy and healthcare, as detailed by MIT Technology Review [24].

4.2.2 Enhanced connectivity

The future of connectivity is set to undergo a profound transformation with the advent of 6G and subsequent technologies, promising unprecedented capabilities for IoT devices and edge computing [25]. Building upon the foundation laid by 5G, 6G is projected to achieve speeds up to 1 terabit per second, marking a hundred-fold increase in speed. This enhancement will facilitate rapid data transmission crucial for real-time applications and high-definition content streaming. The reduction in latency to sub-millisecond levels will prove indispensable for applications like autonomous vehicles, remote surgeries, and augmented reality, ensuring instantaneous responses.

6G's utilization of higher frequency bands, including terahertz waves, will expand bandwidth significantly, albeit requiring advancements in materials and technologies for effective signal propagation, as noted by MIT Technology Review and IoT For All [26]. This enhanced connectivity will enable billions of IoT devices to operate simultaneously, revolutionizing smart cities, industrial IoT frameworks, and sensor networks in sectors such as healthcare, agriculture, and environmental monitoring.

Moreover, 6G's advancements will enhance energy efficiency through new protocols and edge processing capabilities, prolonging IoT device battery life and supporting sustainable operations [27]. Edge computing will benefit immensely from 6G's capabilities, enabling distributed computing and real-time AI at the edge, thereby reducing reliance on centralized cloud servers and enhancing data security and privacy.

Looking forward, future connectivity technologies like 7G hold promise for integrating with emerging technologies such as quantum computing and advanced AI, fostering intelligent communication and enabling transformative applications in virtual reality, autonomous systems, and beyond. This evolution will shape a future where connectivity drives technological innovation and societal progress on an unprecedented scale.

4.3 Emerging evolution: uses and cases

With the evolving space of technology, Refs. [28, 29] mentions that the uses and cases of edge computing has a high likelihood to change.

4.3.1 Smart ecosystem

In today's extremely advanced world, edge computing is a very crucial aspect of smart homes and cities. Internet of Things (IoT) devices have been deployed in smart homes that help monitor the usage of utilities such as water, electricity, and gas, thus making them automated and with accurate readings. This information is then processed at close-by servers avoiding going to the cloud to enable instant billing practices and real-time analytics. IoT technology can be employed in the construction of smart cities which will better manage consumption rates [15, 30]. However, one among the key challenges is how different types of technologies can interact within urban environments. In addition, there are several designs meant for IoT implementations in urban areas. Mobility Edge Computing (MEC), on the other hand, has a potential for detecting critical happenings like calamities or terrorist attacks.

There have been developments in edge computing that allow for checking of user-generated content in real time, facilitating the identification of unusual occurrences [30]. For instance, EVAPS is a platform for video analysis on the edge for public safety. It optimizes the workload distribution for computation between edge nodes and clouds to save energy and also minimize sending unnecessary data. Again, a fog computing-based solution is proposed for smart urban surveillance which can track vehicle speeds and monitor traffic in real-time. Therefore, it's critical to comprehend these applications that demonstrate how efficiency and responsiveness are improved by edge computing allowing more intelligent urban infrastructures (**Figure 5**) [30].

Such smart things as vacuum cleaners that have sensors use edge computing for video analytics, processing huge amounts of mobile information and control connected cars in IoT in the industry (IIoT). On factory floors there is a growing trend of mobile equipment (for example, UAVs, AGVs) which operate together during production, thus making industrial processes better. In applications like industrial

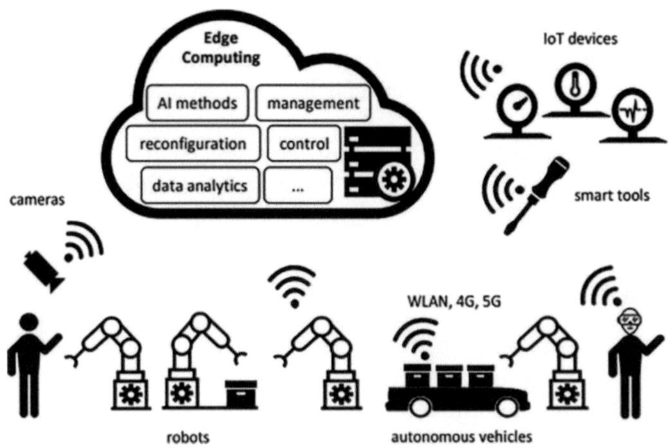

Figure 5.
Industrial use of edge computing. Source: Ref. [30].

robots, low latency and robustness can only be achieved through the use of edge computing. Cooperative robotic arm systems are examples of this joint effort where data analysis and intelligent processing occur at localized points to support manufacturing. Also edge computing encourages surveillance of industrial environments, manages grids, wireless mesh sensor networks besides being on manufacturers' radar nowadays.

4.3.2 Planetary and interplanetary networks

A future of IoT and Edge Computing in space colonization, a merger of people living on other planets and advanced technology- this question is surely gripping. Therefore, to create colonies on the Moon or Mars, and even beyond these celestial objects, it will be absolutely necessary for IoT together with edge computing to establish an atmosphere that can sustain life. In terms of space colonization, IoT systems will have to control vital resources that are necessary for survival. Continuous monitoring of temperature levels, radiation levels as well as air condition using advanced sensors designed to operate under extreme space conditions will make sure that there are safe living environments. This means that during emergencies quick response can be availed through local data processing by use of edge computing without having to wait like in land telecommunication. The importance of IOT and edge computing in water management for space habitats cannot be overemphasized. To achieve self-sustained looping systems with instant analysis of pollutants detection and recycling optimization processes [31], smart water systems must contain nano-sensors that indicate quality level.

To maximize energy capture, distribution, and maintenance prediction through solar panels, energy management will rely on smart sensors that are monitored by edge computing [3, 6, 23]. This assures the availability of continuous energy supply in very harsh space conditions. The agricultural sector will make use of IoT systems for crop health monitoring and control to achieve maximum food production efficiency within habitats maintaining a balance between this and the ecosystem here. As well as that, smart materials enabled IoT devices will be utilized in checking infrastructure integrity in outer space with focus on detecting and proactively addressing structural issues so as to ensure safety and a long life span of critical space infrastructure. In such a case of extraterrestrial settlement, resilient local communication networks shall enhance freedom or autonomy in decision making among colonies hence reducing over-reliance on support from earth while encouraging self-sufficiency.

4.3.3 Personalized experiences

In the realm of technological innovation, edge computing emerges as a transformative force poised to revolutionize personal devices, healthcare, and entertainment [32]. It promises tailored user experiences through its ability to process data swiftly at the edge, reducing latency and enhancing security. According to Ref. [32], edge computing is employed for personalized experiences including

- *Personal devices*: Edge computing accelerates personal devices like smartwatches and fitness trackers, enabling real-time health monitoring and instant notifications. By processing data locally, it fortifies security against breaches, ensuring the integrity of personal information.

- *Healthcare*: Edge computing illuminates healthcare with real-time analytics, empowering practitioners to elevate patient care. It facilitates remote healthcare services and enhances patient surveillance, enabling swift interventions for improved outcomes.

- *Entertainment*: In entertainment, edge computing optimizes gaming experiences by minimizing latency in cloud gaming. It customizes content delivery based on user preferences, offering a personalized and immersive entertainment experience.

4.4 Societal transformation and challenges

4.4.1 Societal impact

Per Ref. [3], Edge Computing reduces the distance of moving data and increases privacy since it reduces the exposure to threats from other sources. It allows instant analysis of a huge amount of data generated by IoT. It permits instantaneous decision-making and protection against data breaches [19, 29]. In smart cities, edge computing optimizes real-time traffic fed by sensors and avoids air pollution while reducing travel time [19]. In this respect, edge computing will help AI applications like real-time language translation or adaptive smart home systems learning from user behavior. Edge computing in healthcare thus supports tele-emergency medical care, which is offered from a distance in boosting personalized provision of medical care. It also makes sure that timely medical monitoring takes place, hence leading to better results on patients. Edge computing reduces the energy used by any IoT device, as the data is processed locally, important for sustaining operations. It maximizes energy use in infrastructures, such as smart grids and green buildings [9, 11], and stimulates novel business ways together with jobs creation opportunities [15].

4.4.2 Ethical and environmental considerations

Together with the expansion of IoT networks and edge computing will come great needs for careful consideration in terms of responsible and sustainable development because of the ethical dilemmas and environmental questions that arise. The principal issues in ethics are related to privacy and safety of data. For example, IoT devices, such as smart home assistants or health monitors, gather enormous personal information and are, therefore, predisposed to unauthorized access and breaches. Stringent safety measures at the level of end-to-end encryption and open data handling practices are important in ensuring confidentiality for the user and mitigating risk [32]. For the growth to be sustainable and sustainable for development, edge computing and IoT networks should be based on deep analysis of a number of moral and environmental hazards involved in this case. They involve significant ethical concerns about privacy and data security because devices that make up Internet of Things—such as smart home assistants and health monitors—collect large volumes of personal data. Of these, perhaps the most important involve the enforcement of stricter safety measures, like end-to-end encryption and making data processing procedures more transparent, in a bid to reduce these risks and give assurance of user confidentiality [28]. These doable steps not only protect user data but also help engender trust and promote the moral use of technology by underscoring the message of tight security processes and better user communication in regard to data practices.

Another critical ethical issue is bias and discrimination. This has led to a number of discriminatory use applications, such as in security and law enforcement. For instance, AI algorithms deployed into the IoT can perpetuate biased outcomes, such as high error levels of facial recognition among people of color [33]. Ensure fairness of AI algorithms through multiple training datasets and frequent audits for bias so that such injustices never take place; this upholds ethics [33]. Moreover, the inherent AI algorithms in an IoT system, especially in safety and law enforcement, can propagate existing biases and consequently be translated into discriminatory acts as high error rates for facial recognition for people of color. Fairness within AI algorithms demand variant datasets during training and routine auditing in the detection and elimination of bias to prevent such injustices and to uphold ethics. Such actions would support ethical applications of AI within IoT frameworks while promoting fairness in output.

Critical elements of deploying IoT systems are transparency and accountability. Clearly indicated lines of how the data shall be accessed, used, or shared should be brought to the users' awareness of its usage. For instance, businesses have to reveal how they apply data from smart thermostats in order to save energy by ensuring there is consent in sharing data. Massive environmental impacts are a result of IoT and edge computing. Carbon emissions are contributed by fabrication and operations on IoT devices and, therefore, demanding design measures for energy saving and use of renewable sources of energy [32]. In addition, e-waste management and resource consumption require designs focused on durability and recycle-ability to help in reducing damages on the environment [33]. These are challenges requiring comprehensive approaches of prime concern to transparency, sustainability in design and manufacturing, ethical AI practices, and proactive environmental stewardship. In this way, we will be able to integrate those concerns into the process of technological development and hence responsibly make use of the transformative capabilities that IoT and edge computing can open for present and future generations.

The IoT system adoption process should be characterized by accountability and transparency regarding access, use, and sharing of consumer data. For instance, businesses will have to obtain customer consent for these operations and be very explicit about the way in which data from smart thermostats is harnessed in order to optimize energy use. In this regard, IoT and edge computing are resource-intensive. Therefore, there is a great impact on the environment in terms of carbon emission during the production and usage of IoT-enabled devices [33]. This calls for the imperative consideration of renewable sources of energy and energy-efficient architecture in the design. Moreover, IoT devices should be designed to enhance durability and recyclability while addressing the challenges of e-waste management and resource use to reduce environmental damage. Needed are comprehensive strategies that premiumize openness, environmentally responsible design and production, moral AI procedures, and proactive environmental stewardship.

4.5 Regulatory frameworks

Connected to that fast growth, the growing influence of IoT and edge computing technologies underlines the global need for standards and regulations. On their own part, these unparalleled technologies bring special benefits but pose huge threats, which should be countered by joint international efforts. Areas that decree global standardization among them are data privacy and security. These include devices like smart home assistants and industrial sensors, which reach out to collect personal information in huge quantities. This data is not secure since its protection has no uniformity over different jurisdictions. This can lead to vulnerabilities like the number of insecure IoT devices attacked by use in cybercrime [34]. Standardizations across the world would ensure that every device meets a certain level of security in order to protect the user's data, retaining trust in these systems [17].

Moreover, bias and discrimination that can occur with the artificial intelligence algorithms in place within IoT systems also call for regulation. If there is not due care paid to design and monitoring, the AI systems will, on their own accord, carry through biases already existing. For example, when facial recognition technology misreads people of color at higher rates, it has led to discriminatory practices [10]. International regulations could force fairness auditing and algorithm transparency to guarantee that AI systems used with IoT applications are fair and not perpetuating inequalities in society [15].

Notably, accountability and transparency in the use of data are equally important. IoT systems have to clearly define their policies governing access, usage, and sharing of data. A user ought to be informed on how his data is being treated and, at the same time, have the ability to control the usage of this data. This can only be effectively done with international regulations standardizing data governance across borders. For instance, a global framework in the same concept as how it has been in Europe might make the General Data Protection Regulation act as a model for handling user data transparently and with accountability [8].

Finally, global regulatory standards for IoT and edge computing technologies are still needed because of their impact on the environment. It is during the manufacture and operation that technological infrastructure makes key contributions to its carbon footprint. International regulations can make use compulsory for energy-efficient components and require that producers minimize e-waste by designing devices for recycling and sustainability. For example, through regulatory requirements, manufacturers can be ensured to produce modular devices that are easier to repair and recycle, hence minimizing their impact on the environment.

4.6 Preparation for the twenty-second century

4.6.1 Innovative policies and collaborations

Harnessing the full potential of IoT and edge computing requires innovative policy-making and robust public-private partnerships. These technologies promise significant advancements across industries and societal sectors, necessitating coordinated efforts between government bodies and private sector entities. Innovative policy-making is pivotal to create regulatory frameworks that foster innovation while safeguarding security, privacy, and ethical use of data. For instance, the European Union's GDPR sets stringent standards for data protection, balancing user rights with the advancement of data-driven services [28]. Similarly, frameworks like the NIST Cybersecurity Framework in the United States promote interoperability among IoT devices, mitigating fragmentation and enhancing user experience [1]. Public-private partnerships play a crucial role in driving technological development and deployment. Collaborations such as the Smart Cities Council leverage private sector innovation and public sector implementation capabilities to accelerate research, pilot new technologies, and scale successful solutions [6]. These partnerships align technological advancements with societal needs, ensuring broad accessibility and maximizing benefits [11].

Infrastructure development is a key focus area for public-private partnerships, where governments provide funding and policy support for IoT and edge computing infrastructure. Initiatives like the European Unions' (EU's) Horizon 2020 program fund projects for smart infrastructure development, while private companies contribute technological expertise [10]. These efforts build essential foundations such as high-speed internet access and edge data centers, facilitating the deployment of smart city solutions like intelligent traffic systems and energy-efficient grids [29]. Moreover, public-private collaborations drive the establishment of industry standards and best practices. The Industrial Internet Consortium (IIC), for example, develops frameworks for secure and interoperable industrial IoT applications, fostering global cooperation and market growth [15]. Standardization efforts ensure that IoT technologies meet high security and performance standards, promoting trust and facilitating international trade.

Investment in education and workforce development is critical for sustainability in IoT and edge computing. The government and the private sector also need to collaborate on training programs and associated certifications for the respective workforce to manage these technologies for deployment [29]. These include, but are not limited to, efforts like the U.S. NICE initiative aimed at closing the gap between the desired skills and the cyber-security/IoT supply, guaranteeing a professional talent pool to grow the industry. Finally, public-private partnerships keep ethical concerns associated with IoT and edge computing in check. In collaborative efforts, guidelines are designed that enable the responsible use of technologies in such manners as data privacy and security, and fairness regarding AI algorithms. Other collaborations, like the Partnership on AI, foster the ethical process of developing AI by bringing together parties to uphold societal values and reduce potential risks.

4.7 Education and skill development

The curriculum/training has to be made that will motivate the coming generation for techno-commercial interrogations in an interconnected and data-driven world, as the IoT and edge computing are evolving very rapidly. Further, these technologies diffuse into different industries; therefore, many diverse skills will be required by individuals to capture their complete potential. Essential technical competencies require knowledge of varied programming languages, including Python or Java, fused with relevant technical experience in tools of data analytics and cloud computing platforms [19]. Cybersecurity training is crucial to safeguard IoT networks and devices against emerging threats.

In addition, it implies technical competence, interdisciplinarity. Data science and machine learning skills help in the analysis of large volumes of data that IoT devices provide [10]. Business acumen brings innovation and value into the IoT ecosystem [29]. It should also form ethical competence like data privacy and fairness in AI algorithms as part of the curricula, to responsibly make use of technology [14]. Critical thinking skills are necessary to enable students reflecting on the impact of IoT deployments on society [35].

Practical skills are developed through hands-on experiences with internships, apprenticeships, and industry collaborations [30]. Competitions and maker spaces further enhance creativity and entrepreneurial thinking [19]. Lifelong learning through professional development programs and certifications will keep professionals current with these developments in the field of IoT [30]. Continuous upskilling for professionals is an important factor in the dynamic job market, as technologies keep changing related to IoT and Edge Computing [35].

4.8 Sustainability and inclusion

Promoting sustainable methodologies and inclusive technology adoption is imperative to guarantee extensive advantages from the Internet of Things (IoT) and edge computing [36]. Sustainable methodologies entail environmental accountability, social justice, and economic sustainability [30]. Regarding the environment, this means reducing the carbon emissions and material consumption of IoT and edge computing technologies by incorporating energy-efficient device designs, enhanced data centers, and the usage of renewable energy resources [3]. Examples include Google and Microsoft, which have pledged to achieve carbon-neutral and carbon-negative operations respectively, setting a precedent in sustainability [36]. Furthermore, sustainable methodologies should consider the full lifecycle of IoT devices, prioritizing durability, recyclability, and responsible disposal practices to mitigate electronic waste and contamination [10].

Technological inclusivity endeavors to address societal inequities by ensuring individuals, irrespective of their backgrounds, can avail themselves of Internet of Things (IoT) advancements [22]. Inclusive design solutions necessitate consideration of diverse user requisites during the developmental phase [10]. For example, in IoT, accessibility features such as voice commands significantly enhance the engagement of users with disabilities [37]. Marginalized groups need to surmount challenges related to affordable internet access and digital education to benefit from IoT innovations (Ibid). Public-private partnerships play a significant part in mitigating these challenges to bridge the digital divide [32]. Inclusive technologies equally aspire to tackle issues of data privacy, security, and ethical usage. Safeguarding user data fosters trust in IoT ecosystems by enhancing transparency in data practices [17]. Ethical directives, such as those provided by IEEE, assist in overseeing responsible AI development to reduce risks such as algorithmic bias [32].

5. Conclusion

Technological and societal progress would be facilitated by IoT and edge computing. A vast network of interlinked IoT devices collects and instantly transmits real-time data. Edge computing accomplishes this near to the data source thereby speeding up decision making and responses [14]. It is this kind of synergy that makes IoT better since it relies on its local data analysis and real-time adaptation, thus making it smarter in the process. For instance, by using IoT sensors coupled with edge computing, smart cities optimize traffic, save energy and enhance public safety. In healthcare also wearable gadgets as well as medical sensors are linked with edge platforms which are used for remote monitoring, personalized treatment and early detection of health issues. This enhances innovation across manufacturing as well as agriculture industries. The prediction maintenance in quality control in smart factories that are IoT enabled along with inventory management which employs the edge computers (Computing). Soil conditions and crop health can be monitored through IOT sensors while edge computing provides insights for precision farming and sustainability in agriculture (Agriculture). Consequently, these advancements have been projected to increase connectivity, efficiency one resource management improvements were made throughout society [19, 38]. Nonetheless there are many ethical concerns that arise from such development that need to be addressed through strong regulations on privacy protection (Privacy). One must encourage a multi-disciplinary approach, which includes computer science, engineering, data science, ethics, policy and social sciences. Collaboration across these sectors lead to innovative solutions while at the same time making sure that there is responsible scaling so as to secure privacy, equality and human rights [18, 25, 29]. It is important therefore for us to provide interdisciplinary education and lifelong learning programs to support development of IoT as well as edge computing technology that will guarantee fair and sustainable outcomes for all people over time.

Author details

Faith Nwokoma* and Cajetan M. Akujuobi
Center of Excellence for Communication Systems Technology Research (CECSTR), Prairie View A&M University, Texas, USA

*Address all correspondence to: faithdgreat4life@gmail.com

References

[1] Madakam S, Ramaswamy R, Tripathi S. Internet of things (IoT): A literature review. Journal of Computing and Communication. 2015;**3**(5):164-173

[2] Abdul-Qawy AS, Pramod PJ, Magesh E, Srinivasulu T. The internet of things (iot): An overview. International Journal of Engineering Research and Applications. 2015;**5**(12):71-82

[3] Mouha RA. Internet of things (IoT). Journal of Data Analysis and Information Processing. 2021;**9**(2):77-101

[4] Kumar D et al. All things considered: An analysis of IoT devices on home networks. In: 28th USENIX Security Symposium (USENIX Security 19). Usenix Associatios; 2019. pp. 1169-1185

[5] Yu W et al. A survey on the edge computing for the internet of things. IEEE Access. 2017;**6**:6900-6919

[6] Zhou Z et al. Edge intelligence: Paving the last mile of artificial intelligence with edge computing. Proceedings of the IEEE. 2019;**107**(8):1738-1762

[7] Mao Y, You C, Zhang J, Huang K, Letaief KB. Mobile edge computing: Survey and research outlook. 2017. Available from: https://arxiv.org/abs/1701.01090

[8] Yousefpour A et al. All one needs to know about fog computing and related edge computing paradigms: A complete survey. Journal of Systems Architecture. 2019;**98**:289-330

[9] Hong CH, Varghese B. Resource management in fog/edge computing: A survey on architectures, infrastructure, and algorithms. ACM Computing Surveys (CSUR). 2019;**52**(5):1-37

[10] Sodiya EO et al. Current state and prospects of edge computing within the internet of things (IoT) ecosystem. International Journal of Science and Research Archive. 2024;**11**(1):1863-1873

[11] Omoniwa B et al. Fog/edge computing-based IoT (FECIoT): Architecture, applications, and research issues. IEEE Internet of Things Journal. 2018;**6**(3):4118-4149

[12] Alam M, Haidri RA, Yadav DK. Efficient task scheduling on virtual machine in cloud computing environment. International Journal of Pervasive Computing and Communications. 2021;**17**(3):271-287

[13] Douch S et al. Edge computing technology enablers: A systematic lecture study. IEEE Access. 2022;**10**:69264-69302

[14] Hewa T, Braeken A, Ylianttila M, Liyanage M. Multi-access edge computing and blockchain-based secure telehealth system connected with 5G and IoT. In: GLOBECOM 2020-2020 IEEE Global Commun. Conf. 2020. pp. 1-6

[15] Silitonga D et al. Edge computing in E-commerce business: Economic impacts and advantages of scalable information systems. EAI Endorsed Transactions on Scalable Information Systems. 2024;**11**(1)

[16] Skok S, Havaš L, Horvat T, Šumiga A. Tesla coil–construction project–educational application. In: EDULEARN22 Proc. Palma, Spain: Edulearn; 2022. pp. 6504-6510

[17] Khattab A, Jeddi Z, Amini E, Bayoumi M. RFID Security. Vol. 11. Springer Berlin Heidelberg; 2017. pp. 27-41

[18] Lavista F. Military Research and Development: The Invention of Packet

Switching. SAGE Bus. Cases Originals: SAGE Publications; 2022

[19] Sunyaev A, Sunyaev A. Internet of Things. Internet Computing: Principles of Distributed Systems and Emerging Internet-Based Technol. Barnes and Noble; 2020. pp. 301-337

[20] De Donno M, Tange K, Dragoni N. Foundations and evolution of modern computing paradigms: Cloud, IoT, edge, and fog. IEEE Access. 2019;7:150936-150948

[21] Andrade L, Serrano M, Prazeres C. The data interplay for the fog of things: A transition to edge computing with IoT. In: 2018 IEEE Int. Conf. Commun. (ICC). IEEE; 2018. pp. 1-7

[22] Firouzi F, Farahani B, Marinšek A. The convergence and interplay of edge, fog, and cloud in the AI-driven internet of things (IoT). Information Systems. 2022;**107**:101840

[23] Chaudhuri A. Internet of Things, for Things, and by Things. Florida, USA: Auerbach Publications; 2018

[24] Gandhi M, Joshi PN. Nanorobots for in vivo monitoring: The future of nano-implantable devices. In: Nanobiomaterial Eng.: Concepts their Appl. Biomed. Diagnostics. Springer; 2020. pp. 227-252

[25] Nguyen DC et al. 6G internet of things: A comprehensive survey. IEEE Internet of Things Journal. 2021;**9**(1):359-383

[26] Courtney J. Taiwan's 6G Future: The Impact of Next-Gen Infrastructure. Worcester Polytech. Inst.; 2024. Doctoral Dissertation. Available from: https://web.cs.wpi.edu/~rek/Projects/6G-C24.pdf

[27] Jha AV, Appasani B, Khan MS, Zeadally S, Katib I. 6G for intelligent transportation systems: Standards, technologies, and challenges. Telecommunication Systems. 2024;**86**(2):1-28

[28] Hassan N, Yau KLA, Wu C. Edge computing in 5G: A review. IEEE Access. 2019;7:127276-127289

[29] Premsankar G, Di Francesco M, Taleb T. Edge computing for the internet of things: A case study. IEEE Internet of Things Journal. 2018;**5**(2):1275-1284

[30] Cui L. [retracted] construction of big data technology training environment for vocational education based on edge computing technology. Wireless Communications and Mobile Computing. 2022;**2022**(1):1060464

[31] Čolaković A, Džubur AH, Karahodža B. "wireless communication technologies for the internet of things," Sci. Engineering and Technology. 2021;**1**(1):1-14

[32] Chang Z et al. A survey of recent advances in edge-computing-powered artificial intelligence of things. IEEE Internet of Things Journal. 2021;**8**(18):13849-13875

[33] Lopez PG et al. Edge-centric computing: Vision and challenges. Computer Communication Review. 2015;**45**(5):37-42

[34] Passian A, Imam N. Nanosystems, edge computing, and the next generation computing systems. Sensors. 2019;**19**(18):4048

[35] Chen J, Ran X. Deep learning with edge computing: A review. Proceedings of the IEEE. 2019;**107**(8):1655-1674

[36] Ranadheera S, Maghsudi S, Hossain E. Computation offloading and activation of mobile edge computing servers: A minority game. IEEE

Wireless Communications Letters. 2018;**7**(5):688-691

[37] Sohaib O, Lu H, Hussain W. Internet of things (IoT) in E-commerce: For people with disabilities. In: 2017 12th IEEE Conference on Industrial Electronics and Applications (ICIEA). 2017. pp. 419-423

[38] Alajlan NN, Ibrahim DM. TinyML: Enabling of inference deep learning models on ultra-low-power IoT edge devices for AI applications. Micromachines. 2022;**13**(6):851

Chapter 6

Perspective Chapter: Is IoMT EHR Integration Leading to Better Patient Health and Well-Being

Steven C. Lindo

Abstract

In light of significant technological advancements in healthcare, there is a need for clear evidence of efficiencies resulting from Electronic Health Records (EHR) and the Internet of Medical Things (IoMT) integration in our healthcare delivery systems. To discover whether these two new technologies have improved the health and wellbeing for patients, seven health and well-being categories were examined. In three of the seven categories for health and well-being, preventative care, accuracy and insights, and remote patient monitoring, benefits were evident, while four categories have no clear evidence of improvements. Fifty-eight percent (58%) of the studies evaluated had evidence of some improvements in health and well-being, with 74% of the studies being from PubMed/Medline and 26% of studies being from IEEE eXplore. The top category was "Accuracy and Insights" with 39%, and the lowest category was "Personalized Treatment Plans" with 1%. The four lowest performing categories were Reduces Healthcare Costs, Personalized Treatment Plans, Increase Patient Engagement, and Efficient Resource Allocation. This study informs our understanding of the advances in health technology as it relates to IoMT and EHRs. The study also exposes the gaps where additional research is needed to address the four lowest-performing categories above.

Keywords: internet of medical things, IoMT, IoT, medical devices, wearable, telemedicine, patient monitoring, health well-being, digital transformation, EHR, healthcare, biotechnology

1. Introduction

The digital revolution taking place in healthcare today is largely driven by two important advances in healthcare. First, medical device modernization has grown using the Internet of Things (IoT) technologies. Second, the exploding of Digital Data comes from EHRs and other digital systems. Both are exposing significant challenges facing this digital transformation era for Health Information Technologies and thus driving the need for efficiencies in patient care.

1.1 Rationale

EHRs have significantly improved patient care by enhancing accessibility and accuracy of patient information [1]. IoMT has emerged as a dependable technology that assists medical personnel in managing patient information and delivering secure digitized healthcare services [2]. IoMT is a connected system combining software applications with medical devices that connect to different healthcare IT systems. IoMT ensures the optimization of healthcare delivery by establishing a secure connection between patients, healthcare service providers, and medical devices, thereby creating a reliable environment for healthcare service provisioning [2]. The assumption then becomes that EHR and IoM integration will improve patient outcomes by enabling continuous monitoring, personalized treatments, and remote care [3]. The expectation is that it will lead to informed decision-making and better health outcomes. At the heart of this "decision-making" is data in the form of health analytics.

2. Background

2.1 The internet of things (IoT)

One of the most significant computer engineering concepts that emerged at the end of the 21st Century is called the Internet of Things, IoT for short. Credit goes to Kevin Ashton [4], MIT's Executive Director of Auto-ID Labs, as the person first to coin the phrase. IoT refers to device-to-device communication where physical devices *communicate* with each other using data communication standards and protocols. A plethora of these systems exist on the market today. They can be found in "smart homes", "smart cities", and many manufacturing innovations.

2.2 IoT components architecture

There are three main components to consider in IoT:

1. The Microcontroller

2. The Data Communication Standards and Protocols

3. The (Smart) Sensors

2.2.1 The microcontroller

First, at the core of the IoT are small microcontrollers. A microcontroller is a tiny computer with an integrated circuit board, a CPU (central processing unit), memory, and input/output interfaces. They are programmable units designed for embedded applications. Meaning it allows you to code your own logic and upload it or embed in microcontroller chips. Three popular microcontrollers I have used for IoT projects include the Raspberry Pi, Arduino, and ESP32.

2.2.2 Data communication standards 101

The second key component of the IoT microcontroller is data communication. A *data communication standard* is a written specification to be followed by manufacturers, developers, and anyone who wants to communicate with another device of the same standard. There are several data communication standards, past, present, and future. The most popular one today is the 802.3 standard for Ethernet. The Open Systems Interconnection (OSI) 7-Layer Model [5] was developed as a guide to explain data communication standards and protocols (**Table 1**).

When it comes to data communication *standards*, they are usually defined at the physical and data link layers, layers 1 and 2, respectively, while application protocols are usually at layers 4–7 of the OSI Model.

Why do we need standards? Standards govern the hardware and software that use them and define the rules for data communications that are needed for interoperability between devices. In short, standards are written for manufacturers. There are a few standards organizations (SO).

- International Standards Organization (ISO)
- International Telecommunication Union (ITU)
- Institute of Electronics and Electrical Engineers (IEEE)
- American National Standards Institute (ANSI)
- Internet Research Task Force (IETF)
- Electronic Industries Association (EIA)

For example, the standards organization EIA (the Electronic Industries Association) authored serial standards RS-232/RS-422A/RS-485. RS-232 is a widely accepted standard that is still used in many implementations today, and because of its popularity, IoT devices almost always have this capability built in. Another example is the standards written by IEEE (the Institute of Electronics and Electrical Engineers) including Ethernet, IEEE 802.3 Wired LAN, and IEEE 802.11 Wireless LAN (WLAN).

2.2.3 IoT data communication standards

The IEEE standards for the Internet of Things (IoT) are called IEEE 802.15.4 [6]. It includes a low-rate wireless personal area network (WPAN) (e.g., Zigbee, Wireless

Layer	Name	Description
7	Application	Client and Server communication
6	Presentation	Data from the application layer is extracted and manipulated in the required format for transmission.
5	Session	Establishes Connection, Maintenance, Ensures Authentication, and Ensures security.
4	Transport	Take Service from Network Layer and provide it to the Application Layer.
3	Network	Transmission of data from one host to another, located in different networks.
2	Data Link	Node to Node Delivery of Message
1	Physical	Establishing Physical Connections between Devices.

Table 1.
OSI 7-Layer Model for Data Communication [6].

HART, and MiWi). The description can be found on IEEE.org. "The architecture framework description for the Internet of Things (IoT) conforms to the international standard ISO/IEC/IEEE 42010:2011. The architecture framework description is motivated by concerns commonly shared by IoT system stakeholders across multiple domains (transportation, healthcare, Smart Grid, etc.). A conceptual basis for the notion of things in the IoT is provided, and the shared concerns as a collection of architecture viewpoints are elaborated to form the body of the framework description".

In 2015, a popular and competing standard was created by the LoRa Alliance. "The LoRaWAN® specification is a Low Power, Wide Area (LPWA) networking protocol designed to wirelessly connect battery operated 'things' to the internet in regional, national or global networks, and targets key Internet of Things (IoT) requirements such as bi-directional communication, end-to-end security, mobility and localization services" [7].

IoT deployments need to figure out which of these technologies is better suited to their application domain. In a comparative study between IEEE 802.15.4 and LoRa, it was found that LoRa-based wireless communication can have an advantage in terms of reliability and complexity of networking. The study found that LoRa has a significantly better communication range and can handle scenarios within multi-floor deployments, reducing the need for repeaters and multi-hop topologies that may be required for other technologies to implement a well-performing network [8]. IEEE 802.15.4, on the other hand, has matured since its inception in 2003 and may be more reliable for short-range deployments. In the healthcare domain, the choice remains to be seen.

2.2.4 Smart sensors

The third component of the IoT is the sensors that are connected to these microcontrollers. Microcontrollers are extensible by design. Extensibility is a systems design principle that measures the ability to add new functionality to the system. Microcontrollers can add sensors, stack hardware, and upload new software anytime we like to enhance our embedded systems. These sensors collect data from the environment and send the data back to the microcontroller for processing.

2.3 Internet of medical devices (IoMT)

The Internet of Things (IoT) has been adopted for medical devices and is labeled IoMT (the internet of *medical* things). In the context of medical devices, IoMT refers to the network of physical devices and sensors embedded with connectivity, software, and other technologies that enable them to collect and share patient information. The connectivity and communication embedded in these medical devices allow near real-time patient monitoring, data analysis, and data-driven decision-making for patients.

IoMT wearable can continuously collect and transmit patient data to healthcare providers. They enable remote patient monitoring, allowing healthcare professionals to track vital signs, track medication efficacy, and other health metrics without the need for the patient to be physically examined. IoMT are also seen as smart medical devices: Devices, such as insulin pumps, pacemakers, and glucose monitors, are now designed with IoMT capabilities. These devices can communicate with a centralized systems to provide near real-time information and insights, with the hope of giving that patient a positive outcome. As these devices become ubiquitous inside and outside medical facilities, the amount of medical data they produce will be zettabytes. As a result, a new communication standard has emerged.

2.3.1 IoMT data communication standards

In healthcare, wearable IoMT device requirements have forced the creation of a new standard, IEEE 802.15.6 – Body area network (BAN) [9], sometimes called wireless body area network (WBAN). The IEEE 802.15.6 standard defines new physical and media access control layer specifications for WBANs. They provide ultra-low-power, low-cost, and short-range wireless communication that operates in or around the human body. The IEEE 802.15.6 standard documents three new specifications:

1. Narrowband (NB),

2. Ultra-Wide Band (UWB) and

3. Human Body Communication – (HBC)

2.3.2 IoMT-EHR integration in the digital transformation era

Why is healthcare's digital transformation and EHR integration relevant? Without it, IoMT would not be useful. The IoMT data collection, data processing, and delivery of the data to an EHR is critical to all data-driven decision-making systems.

Digital transformation (DT) is understood as the organizational change brought about through the utilization of digital solutions, which is becoming more and more compulsory for organizations within the public and private sectors [9]. In simple terms, Digital transformation is a company's "ability" to take their products from printed physical media to digital media. A company's employee's digital maturity is a reflection of how successful they will be at DT.

In healthcare, digital maturity is the extent to which digital technologies are used as enablers to deliver a high-quality health service [10]. Digital maturity builds on existing evidence about digital literacy. In healthcare, this can primarily be captured in the idea of eHealth literacy or the ability of people to use information and communications technologies to improve or enable healthcare. For health systems to support the advancement of digital maturity, staff must be digitally literate and help patients improve their digital literacy. It is important to note, however, that while digital literacy can facilitate digital maturity, digital maturity should also be responsive to the whole patient population and account for their needs regardless of their digital literacy [10]. According to (Kelsey Flott, BA, MSc et al.) [10], digital maturity encompasses not only the resources and ability to use a system but also how interoperable it is with other systems.

The catalyst in the United States that is responsible for driving digital transformation into the US Healthcare System is the landmark legislation (ACA) or the Affordable Care Act (aka Obama Care). This enacted legislation included many mandatory requirements, but for the context of this study, I will focus on electronic health records (EHR) and their meaningful use. Meaningful use is a set of objectives defined by the government for EHR systems. To qualify for incentive payments through the Centers for Medicare and Medicaid Services (CMS) EHR Incentive Programs, eligible providers must demonstrate meaningful use of an EHR System, meaning that the core objectives must be met. EHR, as the name states, is the act of creating electronic versions of patient records and all other activities required to provide care. This includes patient diagnosis, procedures, prescriptions, labs, and referrals. More than 90% of hospitals in the United States adopt certified EHR systems, causing this digital transformation to deliver a data explosion for healthcare. It is estimated that a single patient, on average, will generate 80 megabytes of digital information for their medical records and medical images. According to the US Census data for 2022, approximately 92.1% of all Americans, or 304 million people in the United States, are insured (covered) for healthcare. Therefore, if each person can generate, on average 80 megabytes annually, then this is a "Big Data" problem. Integrate IoMT with your EHR, and now this becomes a big "Big Data" problem.

3. An overview of the study

One problem is that IoMT highlights important challenges that remain unsolved. These include data processing for massive amounts of heterogenous data sets in (near) real-time, new data security, interoperability, and regulatory compliance. I believe new problems will be quickly come to light because these devices are developed by different manufactures and because 100% adherence to standards and specification are difficult to achieve in early stages of technology. Challenges should be expected in:

- Data Communication from lack of adherence to Standards and Protocols.
- Compatibility of software versions affecting features and functions.
- Deployment, maintenance, and upgrades delays.

Therefore, the rationale behind this study is to understand how much of the promise of IoMT is realized and how much of the problem remains in healthcare settings.

3.1 The assertion

If IoMT-EHR integration is improving a patient's well-being, then it should manifest in the following ways.

- *Increased* Remote Patient Monitoring: IoMT devices would allow healthcare providers to remotely monitor patients' vital signs, medication adherence, and overall health status. This would reduce the need for frequent in-person visits and enable early intervention in case of any anomalies or deterioration in health.
- *Improved* Accuracy and Timeliness: IoMT would facilitate real-time data collection and analysis, leading to more accurate and timely insights into patients' health conditions. This enables healthcare providers to make informed decisions promptly, potentially reducing medical errors and improving outcomes.
- *Enhanced* Patient Engagement: IoMT devices empower patients to take a more active role in managing their health. By providing access to their own health data and enabling communication with healthcare providers, patients are more engaged and motivated to adhere to treatment plans and lifestyle changes.
- *Personalized* Treatment Plans: The continuous stream of data from IoMT devices enables healthcare providers to tailor treatment plans to individual patients' needs. This personalized approach can lead to more effective interventions and better outcomes for patients.

DOI: http://dx.doi.org/10.5772/intechopen.1006283

- *Efficient* Resource Allocation: IoMT helps healthcare organizations optimize resource allocation by streamlining processes and reducing unnecessary interventions. This allows healthcare providers to focus their time and resources on patients who need them most, improving overall efficiency in patient care delivery.

- *Preventive* Care and Early Detection: IoMT facilitates proactive monitoring of patients' health status, enabling early detection of potential issues or deterioration. This shift toward preventive care can lead to better health outcomes and lower healthcare costs by addressing issues before they escalate into more serious conditions.

- *Reduced* Healthcare Costs: By enabling remote monitoring, early intervention, and preventive care, IoMT has the potential to reduce healthcare costs associated with hospital readmissions, emergency room visits, and complications from untreated conditions. This can lead to more efficient use of healthcare resources and lower overall healthcare spending.

The aim of the current study is to evaluate these categories in the published literature and identify gaps.

4. Research method

The research method followed a systematic literature search. Search terms were entered into PubMed/Medline and IEEE eXplore search engines. The results were reviewed, and eligible studies were selected.

4.1 Data sources

- PubMed/Medline

- IEEE eXplore

4.2 Search terms

The search strategy combined IoMT and EHR with phases that were identified as benefits of IoMT and EHR(s). The information sources (databases) were searched using the following search terms:

- IoMT Remote Patient Monitoring

- IoMT Accuracy and Insights

- IoMT Increase Patient Engagement

- IoMT Personalized Treatment Plans

- IoMT Efficient Resource Allocation

- IoMT Preventive Care

- IoMT Reduces Healthcare Costs
- EHR Remote Patient Monitoring
- EHR Accuracy and Insights
- EHR Increase Patient Engagement
- EHR Personalized Treatment Plans
- EHR Efficient Resource Allocation
- EHR Preventive Care
- EHR Reduces Healthcare Costs

4.3 Method

4.3.1 Search the data sources

The aforementioned search terms were used to search the data sources. The searches produced 1078 results from PubMed/Medline and 312 from IEEE eXplorer databases, for a total of 1390 search results. The 1390 were filtered by last 5 years and excluded Early Access, Magazines, and Books yielding the filtered results of 647 and 231 studies from PubMed/Medline and IEEE eXplorer, respectively. **Table 2** breakdown the results accordingly.

4.3.2 Apply keyword spotting and KWIC

The abstracts from the 647 filtered results from PubMed/Medline and the 231 results from IEEE were reviewed and categorized into the "category-of-seven-for health-and-well-being". The method for doing this was keyword spotting using keywords in context. Keyword-in-Context (KWIC) is a linguistic technique used to present concordance lines for a corpus. KWIC will show the keyword in its surrounding context. **Table 3** shows the keywords that were used in this method.

Figure 1 shows the results from the keyword "remote patient monitoring" as entered into AntConc concordance tool using KWIC.

In **Figure 1**, you can see that the KWIC results are in four columns:

- file (filename),
- left context,
- hit (search term), and
- right context.

For example, row 7 from **Figure 1** has the following results (**Table 4**).

After reading the left context, hit, and right context, it is clear that this study has evidence of improvements in patient monitoring.

For cases where it was not clear from the KWIC analysis, the abstract itself was reviewed to confirm. For example, row 8 from **Figure 1** shows the following results (**Table 5**).

Database:	PUBMED/MEDLINE
Search query:	
	IoMT Remote Patient Monitoring OR IoMT Accuracy and Insights OR IoMT Increase Patient Engagement OR IoMT Personalized Treatment Plans OR IoMT Efficient Resource Allocation OR IoMT Preventive Care OR IoMT Reduces Healthcare Costs OR EHR Remote Patient Monitoring OR EHR Accuracy and Insights OR EHR Increase Patient Engagement OR EHR Personalized Treatment Plans OR EHR Efficient Resource Allocation OR EHR Preventive Care OR EHR Reduces Healthcare Costs Total Results: 1078 Filter by: • Abstract • Last 5 Years Filtered Results: 647
Database:	IEEE Xplore
Search query:	
	IoMT Remote Patient Monitoring OR IoMT Accuracy and Insights OR IoMT Increase Patient Engagement OR IoMT Personalized Treatment Plans OR IoMT Efficient Resource Allocation OR IoMT Preventive Care OR IoMT Reduces Healthcare Costs OR EHR Remote Patient Monitoring OR EHR Accuracy and Insights OR EHR Increase Patient Engagement OR EHR Personalized Treatment Plans OR EHR Efficient Resource Allocation OR EHR Preventive Care OR EHR Reduces Healthcare Costs Total Results: 312 Filter by: • Last 5 Years • Conference • Journals Early Access (5), Magazines (3), and Books (1) excluded. Filtered Results 231

Table 2.
Search Query Results.

#	Category	Keywords
1	Remote Patient Monitoring	"remote patient monitoring", "telemonitoring", "telehealth"
2	Accuracy and Insights	"accuracy", "insights", "data quality"
3	Increase Patient Engagement	"patient engagement", "patient participation", "patient involvement"
4	Personalized Treatment Plans	"personalized treatment", "customized care", "individualized therapy"
5	Efficient Resource Allocation	"resource allocation", "efficiency", "cost-effective"
6	Preventive Care	"preventive care", "prevention", "early detection"
7	Reduces Healthcare Costs	"reduce costs", "cost savings", "cost-effective"

Table 3.
KWIC Terms.

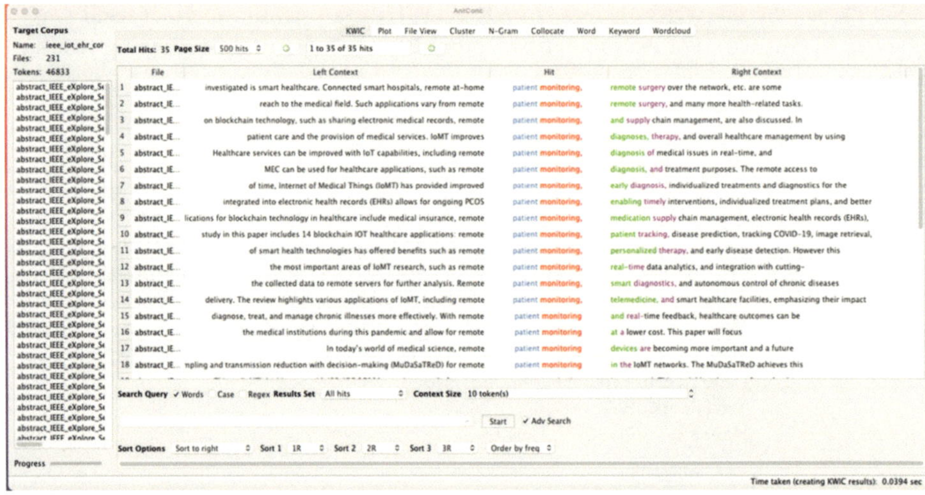

Figure 1.
AntConc KWIC concordance.

File	Left Context	Hit	Right Context
abstract_IEEE_eXplore_Search_Results_export2024.06.08–21.32.13.csv_69.txt	.. of time, Internet of Medical Things (IoMT) has provided improved	Patient monitoring,	early diagnosis, individualized treatments, and diagnostics for the..

Table 4.
Example of KWIC analysis positive for remote patient monitoring.

This process was repeated for all the all the keywords for each of the categories. The KWIC analysis reduced the total number of studies from 647 filtered results from PubMed/Medline and 231 results from IEEE to 596 from PubMed/Medline and 206 from IEEE. **Table 6** shows the results after KWIC was applied.

4.3.3 Analyze and classify

To identify definitive evidence of health and well-being improvements, studies were classified as follows (**Table 7**):

The KWIC analysis results represent the studies with clear evidence for each category (i.e., those classified as "yes"). To confirm, each abstract was searched for indicative evidence related to the categories. Upon further review, if there were ambiguities, these were reclassified from "yes" to "no". **Table 8** shows the final classifications.

File	Left Context	Hit	Right Context
abstract_IEEE_eXplore_Search_Results_export2024.06.08–21.32.13.csv_129.txt	.. integrated into electronic health records (EHRs) allows for ongoing PCOS	patient monitoring,	enabling timely interventions, individualized treatment plans, and better..

Table 5.
Example of KWIC analysis ambiguous for remote patient monitoring.

Keywords with KWIC Results			
Category	**PubMed/Medline**	**IEEE eXplore**	**Total**
Remote Patient Monitoring	97	34	131
Accuracy and Insights	214	100	314
Increase Patient Engagement	45	1	46
Personalized Treatment Plans	5	5	10
Efficient Resource Allocation	55	41	96
Preventive Care	168	24	192
Reduces Healthcare Costs	12	1	13

Table 6.
KWIC Results.

Classification	**Meaning**
Yes	Clear evidence
No	No clear evidence

Table 7.
Classification and meanings.

Classification		
Category	**Yes**	**No**
Remote Patient Monitoring	131	671
Accuracy and Insights	314	488
Increase Patient Engagement	46	756
Personalized Treatment Plans	10	792
Efficient Resource Allocation	96	706
Preventive Care	192	610
Reduces Healthcare Costs	13	789

Table 8.
Classification Results.

5. Results

5.1 Data analysis

Step 1 of this research was to use the database search engine from PubMed/Medline and IEEE eXplore to search for studies related to IoMT and EHR integration. The search results produced 1390 results that were presented in Section 4.3.1 Search the Data Sources. Step 2, the 1390 results were filtered by the last 5 years, excluding magazines and books. Step 3, KWIC concordance and technical analysis were used to identify the studies with evidence of improved health and well-being for each of the seven categories (**Table 9**).

Step 1: Search Results	Step 2: Filtered	Step 3: KWIC Analysis
PubMed / Medline – 1078	PubMed / Medline – 647	PubMed / Medline – 596
IEEE eXplore Lib - 312	IEEE eXplore Lib – 231	IEEE eXplore Lib - 206

Table 9.
Summary of the steps used in this study.

5.2 Results: Summary

Overall, 58% of the studies had evidence of some improvements in health and well-being. Of the 58%, 74% of the studies were from PubMed/Medline, while 26% of studies were from IEEE eXplore. The top category was Accuracy and Insights with 39% of the studies and the lowest category was Personalized Treatment Plans with 1% of the studies. **Table 10** shows the percentages for each category.

5.3 Results: Evidence of improved health and well-being

Figure 2 shows the results from this study. The chart shows the level of evidence found of improved health and well-being in all seven categories.

In three of the seven categories for health and well-being- preventative care, accuracy and insights, and remote patient monitoring – the benefits were evident, while the four categories had no clear evidence of improvements. Fifty-eight percent (58%) of the studies evaluated had evidence of some improvements in health and well-being, with 74% of the studies being from PubMed/Medline and 26% of studies being from IEEE eXplore. The top category was "Accuracy and Insights" with 39%, and the lowest category was "Personalized Treatment Plans" with 1%. The four lowest performing categories were Reduces Healthcare Costs, Personalized Treatment Plans, Increase Patient Engagement, and Efficient Resource Allocation.

The data shows a large gap for the top category, Accuracy and Insights, vs. the lowest categories: Reduces Healthcare Costs; Personalized Treatment Plans; Increase Patient Engagement; and Efficient Resource Allocation; proving that more research is needed in these areas.

It was unexpected that the category for reducing healthcare costs was the second lowest. In 2008, Don Berwick, Tom Nolan, and John Whittington described the Triple Aim of healthcare as the simultaneous effort of improving population

Category	Overall PCT	PubMed / Medline PCT	IEEE eXplore PCT
Remote Patient Monitoring	16.33%	16.28%	16.50%
Accuracy and Insights	39.15%	35.91%	48.54%
Increase Patient Engagement	5.74%	7.55%	0.49%
Personalized Treatment Plans	1.25%	0.84%	2.43%
Efficient Resource Allocation	11.97%	9.23%	19.90%
Preventive Care	23.94%	28.19%	11.65%
Reduces Healthcare Costs	1.62%	2.01%	0.49%

Table 10.
Results Summary.

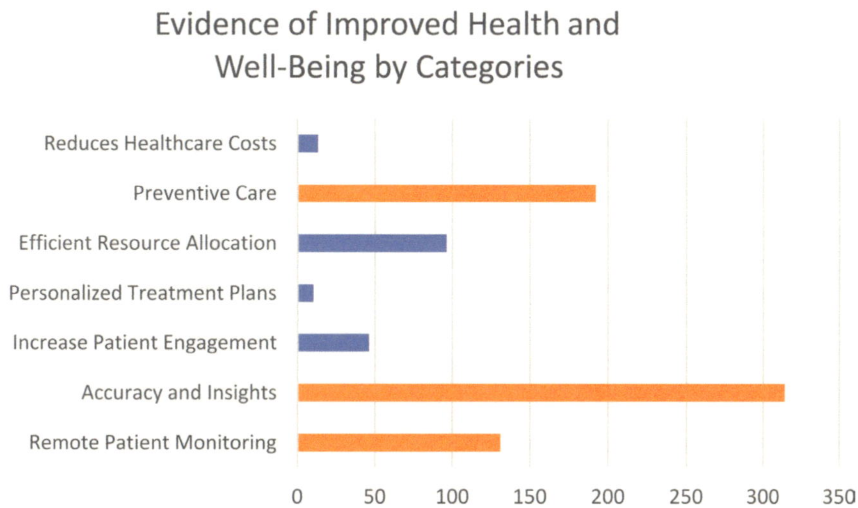

Figure 2.
Results of evidence of health and well-being.

health, improving the patient experience of care, and reducing per capita cost [11]. Since then, the US healthcare system has been in pursuit of the *triple aim*; however, the data from this study shows that only 1.62% of the studies found evidence of reducing healthcare costs, therefore we can conclude that very little consideration is being given to reducing health care costs with regards the IoMT-EHR integration.

Another unexpected result from the study was Remote Patient Monitoring at 16.33%. According to, the remote monitoring of patients using the Internet of Things (IoT) is essential for ensuring continuous observation, improving health-care, and decreasing the associated costs (i.e., reducing hospital admissions and emergency visits). He continues by stating that there has been much emphasis on developing methods and approaches for remote patient monitoring using IoT [12]. Intuitively, this study expected the category for Remote Patient Monitoring to score higher due to the emphasis on IoT and remote monitoring of patients. Instead, Remote Patient Monitoring received a "yes" classification 131 time as opposed to the top category, Accuracy and Insights, at 314, a difference of 183 classifications. This indicates that more research is required to fully understand the true relationships between IoT and the remote monitoring of patients.

It was not surprising that Personalized Treatment Plans are the lowest with only 1.25%. This result can be attributed to where we are currently in the evolution of the healthcare industry. Adapted from (L. Gomathi et al., 2023 7th International Conference on Trends in Electronics and Informatics (ICOEI)) [13] **Figure 3** shows the evolution of the stages of the healthcare industry.

We are currently exiting healthcare 4.0 and entering the next phase. The next phase in this evolution is known as healthcare 5.0. Healthcare 5.0 is characterized by a focus on patient-centered, personalized care that considers a wide range of factors affecting health and well-being [13]. Therefore, the expectation is that Personalized Treatment Plans will increase as we go further into healthcare 5.0. An interesting study could be to use data from healthcare 4.0 to predict the probability of success of healthcare 5.0.

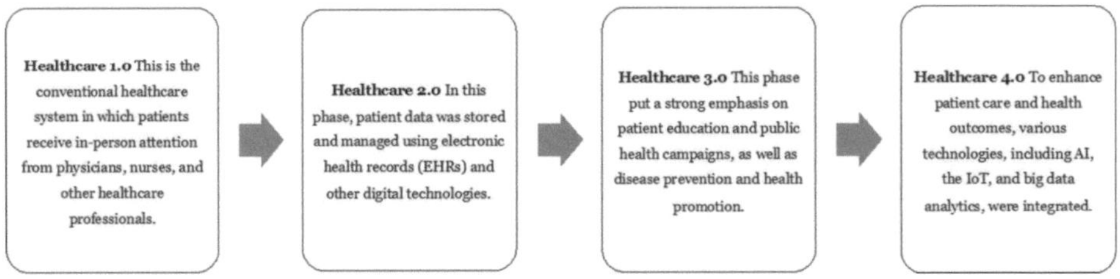

Figure 3.
Stages of the healthcare industry.

6. Conclusion

This research aimed to identify where technology advancements related to IoMT and the integration of EHR delivered better health and well-being for patients. The results from the study identified major gaps in IoMT-EHR integration for patient's health and well-being. The gaps were identified in the following areas:

- reduces healthcare costs,
- personalized treatment plans,
- increase patient engagement, and
- efficient resource allocation.

The study concludes that very little consideration is being giving to IoMT-EHR integration reducing healthcare costs. The study also concludes that more research is required to fully understand the true relationships between IoT and the remote monitoring of patients. Finally, the study recommends consideration be given to healthcare 4.0 and predicting the probability of success healthcare 5.0 will have on Personalized Treatment Plans.

Acknowledgements

The author would like to acknowledge Dr. Lisa M. DeTora, Ph.D., and Dr. Purna Prasad, Ph.D., for guidance, mentoring, and helpful feedback during this study.

Conflict of interest

The authors declare no conflict of interest.

Notes/thanks/other declarations

Special thanks to Dr. Corinne Kyriacou, PhD, MPH for her unwavering support.

Author details

Steven C. Lindo
Master of Science in Health Informatics, School of Health Sciences,
Hofstra University, New York, United States

*Address all correspondence to: steven.c.lindo@hofstra.edu

References

[1] Adeniyi AO, Arowoogun JO, Chidi R, Okolo CA, Babawarun O. The impact of electronic health records on patient care and outcomes: A comprehensive review. World Journal of Advanced Research and Reviews. 2024;**21**(02):1446-1455 Publication history: Received on 13 January 2024; revised on 20 February 2024; accepted on 22 February 2024. DOI: 10.30574/wjarr.2024.21.2.0592

[2] Arefin MS, Rahman MM, Hasan MT, Mahmud M, Medintz I. A topical review on enabling Technologies for the Internet of medical things: Sensors, devices, platforms, and applications. Micromachines (Basel). 2024;**15**(4):479. Published online 2024 Mar 30. DOI: 10.3390/mi15040479, Academic Editor

[3] Osama M, Ateya AA, Sayed MS, Hammad M, Pławiak P, Abd El-Latif AA, et al. Internet of Medical Things and Healthcare 4.0: Trends, Requirements, Challenges, and Research Directions. Sensors. 2023;**23**(17):7435. DOI: 10.3390/s23177435

[4] AshtonK. That 'Internet of Things' thing. RFID Journal. 2009;**22**(1):99-114

[5] ISO/IEC JTC1, Information Technology - Open System Interconnection - OSI Reference Model: Part 1 - Basic Reference Model, ISO/IEC 7498-1. 1994

[6] IEEE Draft Standard for Low-Rate Wireless Networks Amendment: Enhanced High Rate Pulse (HRP) and Low Rate Pulse (LRP) Ultra Wide-Band (UWB) Physical Layers (PHYs) and Associated Ranging Techniques. P802.15.4z/D05. IEEE; Nov 2019. ISBN: 9781504463720. Available from: https://books.google.com/books?id=HZypzQEACAAJ

[7] Yegin A, Seller O. LoRaWAN® L2 1.0.4 Specification (TS001-1.0.4) Authored by the LoRa Alliance Technical Committee Technical Committee Chair and Vice-Chair; 2020

[8] Lidia P, Stylianos T, Georgios M, Dimitrios A. A Comparative Study of LoRa and IEEE 802.15.4-based IoT Deployments inside School Buildings. IEEE Access. 2020. pp. 1-1. DOI: 10.1109/ACCESS.2020.3020685

[9] ISO/IEC/IEEE International Standard – Information Technology – Telecommunications and Information Exchange between Systems -- Local and Metropolitan Area Networks -- Specific Requirements -- Part 15-6: Wireless Body Area Network ISO/IEC/IEEE 8802-15-6:2017(E). New York: IEEE; 2018

[10] Carlsson F, Matteby M, Magnusson J. Digital transformation drift: A population study of Swedish municipalities. In: 24th Annual International Conference on Digital Government Research - Together in the Unstable World: Digital Government and Solidarity (DGO 2023), July 11-14, 2023, Gdańsk, Poland. New York, NY, USA: ACM; 2023. p. 12. DOI: 10.1145/3598469.3598504

[11] Berwick DM, Nolan TW, Whittington J. The triple aim: Care, health, and cost. Health Affairs. 2008;**27**(3):759-769. DOI: 10.1377/hlthaff.27.3.759

[12] Waleed M, Kamal T, Um T-W, Hafeez A, Habib B, Skouby KE. Unlocking Insights in IoT-Based Patient Monitoring: Methods for Encompassing

Large-Data Challenges. Sensors. 2023;**23**(15):6760. DOI: 10.3390/s23156760

[13] Gomathi L, Anand M, Amit T. Industry 5.0 for Healthcare 5.0: Opportunities, Challenges and Future Research Possibilities; 2023. pp. 204-213. DOI: 10.1109/ICOEI56765.2023.10125660